Winning The Game Of College Admissions

5 Strategic Moves To Stand Out In The Crowd

D1445020

Regina Robinson

"Education is the most powerful weapon which you can use to change the world."

– Nelson Mandela

Acknowledgement

It is an honor when one can see the inside of a person's character shine on the outside. I silently lead by example as I allow the manifestation of my work to express my vision, beliefs, philosophies and principles. The footprints I have etched as I journeyed through life have made a tremendous impact in the lives of others as a woman, mother, daughter, sister, aunt, teacher, friend, and coach. This book may have only one official author, however, great work is always accomplished by the multitudes. I am thankful for Shuyinthia Farley-Hembry of Butterfly Works for contributing to the book as she shines the light on standardized testing.

Family is the key to all success. That is why I want to take this opportunity to thank my daughter, Ashlee Robinson for always supporting me as I take time out to help other students. My sister Tarneisha Robinson, my mother Brenda Robinson, my father Willie Robinson, my nephew Robert Millhouse, and my two brothers Brandon and Erron for their support, love, patience, and encouragement. It's awesome to have a supportive family who believes in your vision, supports your dreams, and continues to encourage you daily. Thank you to my editor and friend Nellie Jackson for countless hours of review and unwavering support.

Most importantly, thank you God for walking side-by-side with me on those days when I felt like giving up. You would quietly whisper a reminder, "There are countless students waiting for the answers." I thank you for purchasing this book and hope that you will use it as your guide to successfully prepare for the next phase of your educational journey.

About the Author

Regina Robinson is an award winning International Speaker, Entrepreneur, Amazon best-seller Author, and Educational Coach who is widely known for engaging, motivating, and inspiring high school and college students as she combines genuine inspiration, laughter, and practical principles that will impact change.

After years of teaching, consulting, and coaching in the educational field, Regina continues to provide education, strategies, and accountability for high school families who are excited about their child pursuing higher education but are unsure of how to navigate the college process. She helps students to confidently connect their vision to a plan of action plus execution by providing them with step-by-step guidance in identifying resources to choose the college that is the right fit socially, academically, and financially. She continues to take students to visit colleges on the East Coast, and present college workshops for high schools, community organizations, and churches.

Regina is a member of the Higher Educational Consultant Association (HECA) and the Potomac and Chesapeake Association for College Admission Counseling (PCACAC). As an educational coach, she finds great honor in working with young people. She dedicates her time to staying abreast of current changes in the college admissions process, gaining extensive first-hand knowledge of colleges by attending workshops, professional conferences, seminars and webinars, college fairs, and meeting with admissions counselors and financial aid administrators, touring campuses and getting a "feel" for the environment. When visiting campuses, she has had the opportunity to meet some interesting students, sleep in several resident halls, and learn about programs and scholarship opportunities for students.

Regina has received numerous awards and recognition for her work, including the 2015 PTIO Woman Legacy Builders Award from Cheryl Wood and the 2008 Network for Teaching Entrepreneurship Teacher of the Year Award.

She has been spotlighted in Queens Magazine, and appeared as a featured guest on a host of radio shows including Success in Stilettos, The Nicole Mason Show, Play Time Is Over Radio Show, Stress Less Radio, and No Turning Back. She has served as a featured speaker at the Cheryl Wood Empowers Play Time Is Over Women's Conference 2015 and Women's Empowerment Luncheon, Womanpreneur 2015 Conference, The Biggest Comeback Ever Conference, and a featured keynote speaker for a variety of churches, organizations, high schools and colleges.

Regina Robinson is a graduate of Bowie State University, where she received her undergraduate degree in Business Management and Georgetown University where she earned her Master's Degree in Liberal Studies.

Table of Contents

Introduction

They enter the room feeling shy, nervous, confused and overwhelmed. Questioning why am I here? I take one look at them and immediately, I am reminded of myself. With ease and assurance, I simply tell them *Welcome*. I often see a sense of relief. Now that I have their trust, I simply ask, "Tell me a little about you." Most of the time the parent(s) begins to answer the question. Yes, we call it the helicopter parent. Most students sit in silence waiting for the chance to answer. Some have intriguing answers, others are reserved, and then you have the ones who are confident knowing they have invested in becoming a well-rounded student academically and socially.

If I could go back and whisper to my fourteen-year-old self, I would tell myself that no one could ever stop you in life but YOU. Today I make it a point to utter those very words to every student I come in contact with. Oprah Winfrey once said, "God can dream a bigger dream than you can ever dream for yourself." Dreams are discovered while your eyes are closed, but in order to make them a reality you have to open your eyes everyday with the determination that achieving your dreams are possible. The distance between your dreams becoming a reality will seem difficult; you will experience some setbacks and failures, but I promise along your journey you will discover THE WINNER IN YOU!

Here are four principles that will strategically propel you forward as you unveil your WHY in life...

- **Success Requires You To See Beyond Today...** Don't allow today's worries to cloud your judgment of tomorrow's possibilities. Remember it is not about the fall as much as it is about your tenacity to get back up. Success requires your willingness to never give up on you, create possibilities, and embrace all opportunities.

- **Opportunities Are Not Given, They Are Made...** Just because some students come from other schools in the top of their class doesn't mean they are smarter than you. It simply means they are willing to sacrifice today in order to prepare for tomorrow. What that means is they are willing to miss some of the games, parties, after school activities, and hanging out – just to name a few in exchange for creating opportunities that will position them for their next level.

- **The Resilience To Achieve Your Full Potential...** On the road to your full potential you will encounter obstacles along the way; however, remember they are just detours/not a stop sign. What choice will you decide to make? The difference between you and someone else will be your resilience to want it more. You must answer the question: Am I willing to do the unexpected in order to pursue my dreams? It's important to put in the work today in preparation for tomorrow.

- **Never Give Up On You...** Your determination to succeed must always outweigh your desire to give up. You must believe in yourself more than you believe in failure. Remember it is never an option to give up.

Everyone is in a race to the finish line that is college. In the haste of it all it's important to know what moves to make strategically to not just SHOW UP for the game, but to position yourself to WIN the game.

Right about now you are receiving an influx of mail, information and people telling you to do this and do that. That all sounds great; however, what about where and how to start? Whether you are a middle or high school student trying to figure it all out, remember it is never too early or too late to take action.

This book is designed to help you enhance your high school-to-college experience by providing you with the resources, answers and guidance needed to strategically navigate the college admissions process with ease, determination and confidence. The tips and strategies in this book are what led to Suited 4 Success helping our students earn over $10 million dollars in scholarships and grants.

EVERY DAY, SHOW UP for your greatness and never stop moving towards your destiny.

1 College Research

- 5 Strategic Moves To Stand Out In The Crowd

2 College Visits

3 One Size Does Not Fit All "SAT vs ACT"

4 Crafting Your Unique Story

5 Financing Your Education

Strategic Move 1

College Research

The college research process can be intimidating and overwhelming. One of the most important aspects of starting the college process is being true to you. If you are anything like how I was in high school you're still unsure about your exact plans. At this very moment, you don't have to decide what you want to do with the rest of your life. What you must do is decide to give yourself permission to embrace as many opportunities as possible in life as you discover what really interests you.

With over 4,000 college options to choose from finding the one that fits can be a little scary. Don't worry we will go on a journey together to discover how to navigate the many different options available like books, research websites, college fairs, college visits, guidance counselor and parent nights.

When comparing the supply and demand of students to counselors we know which one is suffering. Unfortunately, most public high schools nationally on average have a counselor-to-student ratio of 500 to 1. And that number continues to rise across the nation. That is why I am passionate about helping students to strategically navigate the college admissions process. In this book I share all my resources to ensure your success. Think of this book as your Guided Problem Solver (GPS).

Here are some key areas to become familiar with as you begin your college research to unveil options that seem right for you...

Public University: is a university that is predominantly funded by public means through a national or subnational government, as opposed to private universities (expect larger enrollment, a wide array of academic programs and a diverse student body).

Private College: is an independent school that sets its own policies and goals, and is privately funded and generally smaller than public or private universities. (the average enrollment at private colleges is only 1,900 students; private universities, by contrast, can have over 30,000 students).

Two-Year Community College: is an educational institution that provides tertiary education and continuing education supplemental to traditional universities and colleges. Two-year colleges (also known as junior or community colleges) usually offer an Associate's Degree.

Four-Year College: is an educational institution that usually offers a Bachelor's Degree; they often are entirely undergraduate institutions, although some have Graduate School Programs.

College: constituent unit of a university, furnishing courses of instruction in the liberal arts and sciences, usually leading to a Bachelor's Degree.

University: is an institution of higher learning with teaching and research facilities typically including a Graduate School and professional schools that awards Bachelor's, Master's and Doctorate Degrees.

Liberal Arts College: is a college with an emphasis on undergraduate study in the liberal arts and sciences that aims to impart a broad knowledge and develop general intellectual capacities, in contrast to a professional, vocational, or technical curriculum.

Think about who you are and what you want to get out of your college experience. Your interest and personality traits that affect you should be the driving force in guiding your research.

Remember staying true to you is key. So it's time for you to take the lead in unveiling what special talents you possess, the type of learning style you enjoy, and the type of experience you want to gain from college.

Here are some factors to consider in discovering what will make you happy...

- Do you like quiet, natural settings or lots of excitement
- Do you want to be close or far from home
- What values are most important to you
- Is cost a factor
- What activities, clubs, sports and organizations are you looking to continue in college
- What unique qualities are you looking for in a school

By answering these questions you create a more focused research criteria.

With so many colleges to choose from how do you identify what college is best for you? Every college has unique qualities that set them a part from other schools. Here are some key things to consider when doing research: location, type of environment, and school.

Here are some factors to consider as you expand your college research...

Suburban Colleges: Are located in small cities, large towns, or residential areas near large cities with populations between 25,000 and 200,000

Note: Suburban campuses often provide students with access to both outdoor activities and entertainment options, museums and concerts

Examples of suburban colleges include:
- University of Maryland College Park
- University of Virginia
- North Carolina A&T University

Rural Colleges: are colleges that are located in the country often with access to wilderness areas, farms and towns with a population of less than 25,000 people

Note: Rural colleges are great for students who love the outdoors and are looking for community

Examples of rural colleges include:
- University of Maryland Eastern Shore
- Bucknell University
- Washington College

Urban Colleges: are located in large cities with populations of 200,000 or more

Note: Urban colleges are good environments for outgoing students who like to explore and interact with all different types of people and cultures, and the city life

Examples of urban colleges include:
- New York University
- Northeastern University
- UCLA

Choosing an in-state school does not always mean lower tuition price. It very well depends on the school. In fact there are some out-of-state schools that can have a lower cost than an in-state school.

Now is the time to decide if you're looking for a smaller environment or in fact would like to attend a larger school. There are a number of factors to consider when deciding between a smaller or larger school. Small schools offer smaller classroom sizes, close-knit communities, student engagement and more personalized attention. Larger schools tend to have larger classrooms, less of a community feel, and the opportunity to remain private. When doing your research look at each college individually with the understanding that they all offer a variety of different dimensions, but share common characteristics.

The question becomes which one is more appealing to you...

Small Colleges: have fewer than 5,000 students

Note: Some examples of private colleges are Spelman College, Colgate University, and Reed College; some small public colleges are SUNY and Delaware State University

Medium Colleges: have between 5,000 to 15,000 students

Note: Some schools like Yale University, North Carolina A&T State University, Howard University, Duke University, are all medium-sized

Large Colleges: more than 15,000 students

Note: Some schools like New York University, University of Pennsylvania and University of Maryland College Park, are all large colleges

Next up, academics! This should be ranked high on your list when researching colleges. However, it is just one component of the experience. Now the question to ask: am I looking for a school that focuses only on undergraduate teaching and/or research? Most colleges have an academic page for each department so be sure to visit and gain insight on your program of interest. As you move forward don't worry if you're not sure at this time. Research schools that have an array of majors or that offer a liberal arts education. This will grant you the opportunity to explore your interests within a strong academic foundation before making a final decision.

Academic Major: is the academic discipline in which an undergraduate student formally commits. A student who successfully completes all courses established in an academic major qualifies for an undergraduate degree

Here are a few questions that will help in your research as you uncover the best academic environment for you...

- What are your greatest academic strengths and weaknesses
- Do you prefer learning in an environment that offers small discussion group or in a large lecture class
- What is your favorite subject
- How well do you handle academic struggles and pressures
- Are you currently taking Advanced Placement classes
- Do you have any learning challenges or concerns

Don't panic! You don't have to lock yourself into a major at this moment; generally, you begin your major in sophomore year. I suggest if you're unsure, utilize that time to explore classes that will help you determine a major to pursue. Can I share my personal anecdote? I started out as a Nursing major, then I switched to an Education major, and then decided to be a Business and Education major. In the end I graduated with a Business degree.

Now that you have discovered the schools that offer excellent academics, this does not mean they automatically go on your college list. There are other contributing factors to consider.

Let's examine some areas that are often overlooked in the college research process...

Cost: cost should be a part of the decision making process in your research, but not the deciding factor on whether or not to apply to the dream school you love – don't count out a school until you have received a financial aid package. Do your research and focus on the schools that offer substantial financial aid and/or merit scholarships. Be sure to visit school websites and take time to utilize their financial aid calculator. (For more details see Strategic Move 5).

Retention Rate: is the percentage of a school's first-time, first-year undergraduate students who continue at that school the next year. As many as 1 in 3 first-year-students won't make it back sophomore year. The reasons range from family problems and loneliness to academic struggles and a lack of money.

Graduation Rate: most students enter college with a four-year plan. However, changing or adding majors, retaking classes or taking time off for personal reasons can quickly extend that plan to five or more years.

College Selectivity: is a measure of how difficult it is for students to get admitted. Much of the anxiety about "getting in" comes from students who are applying to colleges that admit few students. Having a 4.0 and high-test scores is no guarantee for highly selective schools with admissions rates of less than 15%.

Study Abroad: allow students to complete part of their degree program through educational activities outside of the United States.

Diversity Of Students: most college websites provide statistics about student ethnicity and the percentage of international students.

I'm sure by now you're beginning to understand why it is important to not wait until senior year to begin researching and navigating the college process.

We have a few more stops to go in the college research process...
     If you're an athlete looking to continue playing sports at the collegiate level you have to decide on Division I, II or III. Not everyone is cut out to play at this level. In your research look for schools that offer intramural or club sports.

College Athletics or College Sports: encompasses non-professional, collegiate and university-level competitive sports and games requiring physical skill, and the systems of training that prepare athletes for competition performance. For more information visit **www.ncaa.org**.

     If you're a student who enjoys being actively involved in extracurricular activities and that is a priority for you, it is important that during your research you look for schools that offer the clubs and groups that interest you. Although academics, cost and athletics can be at the top of the list for some, activities play an important role for others as it often provides a social outlet.

Extracurricular Activities: fall outside the realm of the normal curriculum of school or university education, performed by students.

As you are aware there are thousands of colleges in the U.S., all of which may offer a number of ways to apply. Do your research on each school's policy.

When doing your research it is important to determine what application process your schools are utilizing...

Common Application: (informally known as the Common App – opens August 1st) is an undergraduate college admission application that applicants may use to apply to any of 693 member colleges and universities in 48 states and the District of Columbia, as well as in Canada, China, and many European countries. **www.commonapplication.org**

The Common Black College Application: does away with the repetitiveness of traditional college applications by using one application for forty-six separate Historically Black Colleges and Universities. **http://commonblackcollegeapp.com/**

Universal College Application: (also known as the Universal College App – opens July 1st) is a US-based organization, which provides college admission applications that allows students to apply to any of the participating colleges.
https://www.universalcollegeapp.com/

There are different ways you can apply to colleges – here are some options...

Regular decision (RD): (usually has a January deadline and a March or April notification)

Early Action (EA): you can get accepted, denied or deferred and you are not obligated to accept if you get offered a spot – some early action schools have restrictions when applying to other colleges like Harvard, Princeton, Yale, Stanford, and the University of Notre Dame (usually has a deadline of November 1st or 15th and a notification in December/January)

Early Decision (ED): is a binding contract (you plus your school counselor and parent sign) meaning you agree if you get accepted upfront to enroll even before seeing your financial aid offer (usually has deadlines of November 1st and a notification in December/January)

Rolling Admissions (RA): range of time from fall to spring in which a student can apply

Make sure to do your research and clearly understand the pros and cons of each option before choosing which one best suits you. Keep in mind if you choose early action or early decision you must be prepared with your test scores, recommendation letters, essay(s) and grades. First impressions are lasting impressions. Position yourself to stand out in the crowd.

Now that we have covered the above areas, let's discuss another important factor, which is researching schools to ensure you meet the outlined criteria for admissions.

Here are key areas you need to examine when determining your chances at the schools you're considering...

Grade Point Average (GPA): is a number representing the average value of the accumulated final grades earned in courses over time calculated by adding up all accumulated final grades and dividing that figure by the number of grades awarded.

Standardized Testing: almost every school accepts the SAT/ ACT. Over the years, a number of schools have decided that testing is not a definitive way to profile students so they have decided to go test-optional (see Strategic Move 3 for more details).

Test-Optional: admissions policy means some applicants can choose not to submit SAT or ACT scores. The rules vary from college to college. This option comes at a price. You have to determine if you're willing to pay.

The game doesn't stop here. Let's take it one step further to determine what type of applicant you are in the eyes of the college: Likely, Target or Reach. It is important to see how you match up with your schools as it relates to your academics and standardized testing. Most schools publish data on their 50% range of accepted applicants; the question is how do your credentials measure up?

The number one problem I encounter when meeting with students is that their college list is all too often un-balanced. The golden rule is creating a balanced list of between 5 – 8 colleges; however most students often have more Reach than Target or Likely schools. I never want to be the bad guy, so I try and let them down easy by saying, *let's make some minor adjustments.*

If you were applying to a total of seven schools we would break your list down as follows...

Likely – 3 schools (extremely confident – 80% chance of admissions)

Target – 2 schools (still not sure – 30-80% chance of admissions)

Reach – 2 schools (stretch – below 30% chance of admissions)

Note: a school with an admissions rate below 15% will be considered a Reach school for all students regardless of their scores and GPA.

Whatever schools you choose, be sure that you can see yourself as a student at all of them.

Now that you have finalized the college research process take a step back and objectively look at your results. Keep your expectations realistic. Remember the number one priority in this process is discovering what makes you happy.

Remember to use your time wisely as you strategically navigate through the college admissions process from submitting applications, to college visits, to testing, to essay writing, to completing scholarships and financial aid. The process takes time, organization and most importantly commitment. Students are accepted on a first-come basis. Don't delay and miss your opportunity, as schools have less space for new students. The sooner you submit your application the quicker you will hear back from schools with an answer.

Don't hesitate to ask for help from your school counselor or contact us if you need assistance.

The Top 5 Ways To Avoid Stress In The College Process

Maintain Balance

Keep Your Eyes On The Prize

1. Keep Your Space Organized

- Keep a file folder strictly for college
- Make copies of all of your assignments

2. Manage Your Time

- Procrastination is a thief of the future
- Create the best system that works for you

3. Maintain Balance

- Manage your time between school, extra-curricular activities, the college process and fun
- Don't forget to make time for you

4. Meet deadlines

- Don't put off until tomorrow what you can do today
- A deadline is just that, a deadline. Always start your work ahead of time

5. Keep Your Eyes On the Prize

- Don't let the anxiety of getting into the college of your choice stop you from trying to get in
- It is very important for a student to find a major they are passionate about and will be able to make money
- Don't allow the stress of the process to restrict you from enjoying your experience
- Maintain academic success... Keep up your grades
- Do your research and you will find the right college for you

Freshman Checklist

Are You Ready?

Plan Your Path to College

August
- Start off on the right foot with your grades. Colleges will look at your GPA from all four years of High School.

September
- Stay organized by using a planner or download a planning app.
- Work with your school counselor to select courses that are recommended for college preparation and required for graduation.

October
- Talk to your parents about a college savings plan to help cover college costs.
- Develop an activities resume to keep track of your participation in extracurricular activities.

November
- Talk to your parents about your plans for the future. Discuss your personal and academic strengths and your plan to reach your goals.
- Begin having a conversation about financing your education with your family.

December
- Research colleges online that interest you and create a list of what you like most and least about each school.

January
- Research financial aid and grants you are eligible for.

February
- Read in your free time to develop a strong vocabulary, which is an important component in college entrance exams.
- Research careers related to subjects that most interest you.

March
- Meet with your school counselor to select your classes for 10th grade and think about what classes you need to take to prepare for college.

April
- Search for summer camps in your area of interest at colleges you want to attend.

May
- Build relationships with teachers, counselors, coaches, and community members who can help with reccomendations in the future.
- Learn about the world of work through job shadowing, volunteering, or interning this summer.

June
- Start a summer reading list.
- Participate in hobbies and activities related to your career interests.
- Don't be afraid to alter your career goals as you learn more about yourself and the world of work, but remember to keep your goals attainable.

For more helpful resources visit: www.suited4success.org

Sophomore Checklist

Are You Ready?

Plan Your Path to College

August
- Stay organized with a planner to help you throughout the year.

September
- Start applying for scholarships.
- Find a mentor who can help you through high school to prepare for your college experience.
- Plan for PSATs and college entrance exams.

October
- Attend a college fair in your area.
- Start completing your applications and essays.
- Join a club or get involved in an activity at your school or in your community.
- Talk to friends and family about their college expriences.

November
- Begin recording a resume of your accomplishments and academic achievements.
- Meet with college representatives who visit your school to get more information on colleges you are interested in.

December
- Talk with your school counselor about college admission requirements to make sure you take the right classes.

January
- Continue to research financial aid options and align them with your colleges of interest.

February
- Start thinking about what majors and college programs interest you the most and begin to research them.

March
- Meet with your school counselor to ensure your junior classes meet college admission requirements.

April
- If possible take an AP class or two to better prepare for college.
- If you are taking a vacation, be sure to visit as many college campuses as possible.

May
- Ask your school counselor if there are any summer camp programs you could attend to help get you ahead.
- Compare careers that interest you most.

June
- Talk to your parents about college expenses and make a plan to cover them.
- Participate in a summer job or activities that are related to your career interests.

For more helpful resources visit: www.suited4success.org

Juniors Checklist

Are You Ready?

Plan Your Path to College

August
- Review your high school courses and activities. Colleges are looking for challenging course work, strong grades, and extracurricular activities.

September
- Browse college websites and create a preliminary.
- List 10-15 colleges you would like to attend.
- Talk over your list with your parents and high school guidance counselor and begin to narrow it down.
- Begin studying for the winter SAT and ACT.
- Attend college fairs and parents' nights in your area.

October
- Research AP or college courses you might take.

November
- Review the eligibility requirements for federal and private student loans.
- Begin having a conversation about financing your education with your family.
- Plan to take the winter SAT and ACT tests.
- Attend financial aid nights in your area.

December
- Research and apply for scholarships.

January
- Research private scholarships and other aid programs. Check with your parents' employers, local membership organizations, or programs related to your intended course of study.
- Mark your calendar with dates for future tests.

February
- Schedule an exam prep course, if necessary.

March
- Start visiting the top six schools on your list. Schedule an admissions interview and an overnight stay. If possible stop by the school's financial aid office to collect information.

April
- Attend a spring break college tour.

May
- Take the SAT and/or ACT.
- Mark your calendar with the dates for future tests.

June
- Continue researching organizations that award scholarships to graduating seniors. You may need to apply for them the summer after your junior year.
- Begin preparing essays for admission and scholarship applications.

For more helpful resources visit: www.suited4success.org

Senior Checklist

Are You Ready?

Plan Your Path to College

September
- Meet with college admissions representatives visiting your school.
- Create a list of important application and financial aid deadlines.
- Request recommendation letters from your teachers, guidance counselors.

October
- Take the SAT and/or ACT if necessary.
- Start completing your applications and essays.
- Revisit your top three schools and speak face to face with current students and faculty.
- Continue applying for scholarships.
- Gather the data needed for the Free Application for Federal Student Aid (FAFSA).

January
- Continue waiting to receive acceptance and financial aid award letters from the schools you have applied to.
- Check to see if you need to send mid-year transcripts to your prospective schools.

February
- Start planning for AP exams.
- Look for your Student Aid Report (SAR) in the mail, Pay particular attention to the Expected Family Contribution (EFC) and discuss it with your parents and family.

March
- Start comparing the financial aid packages and acceptance letters.

April
- Make a final decision and prepare to send in a deposit by the deadline.

November
- Take the SAT and/or ACT one final time, if necessary.
- Wait to recieve financial aid letters from your colleges of choice.
- Finalize your remaining college applications.

December
- Contact the financial aid office at your chosen school to make certain your application is complete.

May
- Take AP examinations. Write thank you's to the people who wrote you letters of recommendation.

June
- Celebrate your high school graduation!

For more helpful resources visit: www.suited4success.org

Strategic Move 2

College Visits

Why is it that students pick colleges sight unseen? Parents I have one question for you, "Would you purchase a home that you could not see inside of first?" I'm sure your answer was "No". Then why are we (I am a parent also) willing to make such a large investment before we explore up close and personal, how our money will be spent?

College visits are one of the most intriguing parts of the college process. No website, guidebook, or testimonial can replace walking around on campus and seeing with your own eyes what the school has to offer. I take students on college tours yearly and most students go with a favorite school in mind. When I ask why the school is their favorite, most of them don't have a clear answer. Then others have the following answers; my friend attends and loves the college, they have a great football team, the pictures on the website look great, it's my parents' alma-mata, or my boo goes to that school just to name a few. Some students, after visiting quickly realize it is not the school for them. It is best to discover this early than to arrive on your first day as a freshman and realize you made the wrong decision – No Refunds.

Visiting college campuses affords you the opportunity to talk with students, faculty, and financial aid and admissions officers. It allows you to get a glimpse of the campus by walking around the yard, sitting in on classes and visiting the dorms.

Visiting every college may not be possible, that's why it is important to...

Step 1: Create a preliminary list of about 15 – 20 schools

Step 2: Do your research by visiting college websites and reviewing their brochures

Step 3: After researching narrow your list down to the top 10 schools

Step 4: Now it's time to begin your college visits

One way to discover the culture and community of a school is to show up on campus and stand in the middle looking around as if you are lost. You can unveil a lot in how people respond to you.

Now do not do the unthinkable and show up to a college campus without doing your research; explore the college website, review any materials you received and most importantly prepare your questions to ask during your visit.

Ask questions that will give you insight into what the college has to offer...

- Is admission need-blind or need-aware
- What's the freshman-to-sophomore retention rate
- What is the average class size and student-to-faculty ratio
- Are most classes taught by professors or by teaching assistants
- What types of meal plan does your school offer and how is the food
- Does your campus offer a diverse make up of students
- What activities are most popular on your campus
- How many quiet spaces are there for studying?
- How many students are commuters and how many are campus residents
- What career advising services are offered

If you can set up an academic meeting be sure to ask the following questions when meeting with professors or sitting in on a class...

- What are some hands on Experiential Learning assignments students engage in
- What's the average amount of years it takes for a student to graduate
- Are accommodations for diverse learning styles fostered
- How engaged are the professors with the students
- How often do TAs teach classes
- How involved are academic advisors
- Does the school have access to any additional library collections (local or other school libraries)?

Your college experience has a lot to do with your environment so familiarizing yourself with housing and campus amenities is key...

- What's the campus crime rate like
- How does the college ensure student safety
- Does the campus have its own security force and how often do they patrol
- How are residence halls secured
- Is housing guaranteed all four years
- Is the campus completely WiFi accessible

Maximize your visit with the following college checklist...

- If you are unable to attend colleges on your own as a family join an organized college tour. Our organization hosts a college tour every year and one of the biggest concerns families have is taking time off to travel, and the investment that it cost for an entire family to travel to multiple states.

• Schedule your visit while schools are in session so you can gain a clear view of student life on campus. Check with each school to schedule a guided tour of their campus. Scheduled visits and open houses give schools an opportunity to roll out the red carpet and share the glitz and glamour of what their school has to offer. Also, check out the flyers and bulletin boards and pick up a school newspaper to get a sense of what's going on.

• Contrary to belief, the admissions counselors are not the only experts you want to speak with while visiting campuses. In fact, current students are the true experts, because if they have a problem or complaint, they will most likely share it with you. Also they won't be shy about sharing the love they feel for their school. Now don't just stop a student without having your specific questions ready.

When visiting campus stop a student and ask the following questions...

• I received a lot of acceptances why should I choose your school

• What makes this school unique

• How accessible are professors

• How has attending this college changed who you are as an individual

• If you had to change anything about this school what would it be

• Does this feel like a home away from home

- Stop by the Admissions Office and introduce yourself. Meet with a counselor if possible to discuss your interests and share a little about your research and experience while visiting the school. Don't forget to ask for a business card so you can follow-up via email. When you return home send an email thanking the counselor for taking the time to meet with you. Be sure to mention one thing that stood out to you about your time together. Also, remember to fill out an inquiry card while visiting. Colleges keep track of students who demonstrate interest by visiting their campuses.

- If given the opportunity to have on-the-spot interviews don't pass it up. I know you didn't prepare. My answer, "You woke up ready. Remember you never have to practice being you".

- A number of schools offer overnight programs to connect you with a current student in your field of interest. Take the opportunity to experience first-hand campus life, dorm life, and what it would be like as a student at one of your desired schools. Not all schools offer overnight visits; however, most will allow you to visit and sit in on a lecture.

- When visiting college campuses take notes or utilize your voice recorder to outline the pros and cons of each school. Why? After visiting a number of schools they will all begin to look and feel the same. Every school is unique in it's own way and you want to capture what that is for you.

Here are few questions you should ask yourself and record your answers...
- How did you feel when walking around campus
- When interacting with random students did they seem inviting and helpful in answering your questions
- How did you feel about the size of the campus
- When walking around did you feel safe
- Are there stores nearby where you can purchase supplies and groceries
- If you're asking the question: How will I know if this is the school for me? I want to say it will be like love at first sight – for some that is true, you will get butterflies – it's possible, and you get the feeling that this is too good to be true.

After your visits take time to weigh the pros and cons and begin building a solid college list.

Some important factors to consider ...
- Getting in an early visit to a potential top choice school is important if you're considering early application deadlines.
- Note how the students interact with one another. Do they greet people as they walk across the campus? Does the school showcase school spirit? Do most students live on or off campus? Do they offer Greek life? These are all factors that can influence the social life on campus.
- An important question is: Does the school offer a plethora of academic opportunities, internships and study abroad programs that interest you? I recommend students who participate in our college bound programs

to consider two academic areas of interest and we work to create their college list. You might ask why? Most students change their major at least one time while in college. You don't want to have to change colleges simply because they may not offer your new program of interest.

Listen to your gut and take notes: Did the campus have a comfortable feel? Did the campus remind you of home? Did you feel a sense of community on the campus from students and faculty? Was it all you imagined it would be?

Many colleges invite their accepted candidates to spend a few days on campus before the May 1st deposit enrollment date. Utilize this as an opportunity to make in-depth comparisons between your top three colleges.

Don't get overwhelmed during college visits remember to have fun! Enjoy the moment and the time spent with family and friends. I can still remember all the fun I had in high school on a college trip. We laughed, joked, over-slept and almost missed the bus; but most importantly we enjoyed our time learning about the different schools we visited. Which in the end turned out to be one of the schools I attended. The ultimate goal is to find the one school you can call home for four years.

Strategic Move 3

One Size Does Not Fit All
"SAT vs. ACT"

Written by: Shuyinthia Farley-Hembry,
Butterfly Works

What is the SAT / ACT and why are they important? The SAT / ACT are both entrance exams used by most colleges and universities to make admissions decisions. The idea (in theory, at least) is to provide colleges with one common criterion that can be used to compare all applicants. The weight placed on the SAT and ACT scores vary from school to school.

The SAT is given seven times throughout the year in January, March, May, June, October, November, and December. The ACT is given six times throughout the year in February, April, June, September, October, and December.

Scenario! You walk into class and your guidance counselor announces that you're about to register for the upcoming SAT or ACT exam. Immediately, you become nervous.

Your palms begin to sweat and you're full of questions and anxious thoughts...

- What is the SAT
- Why are we registering for it today
- Do I have a choice
- I'm not ready
- I haven't taken trigonometry yet
- Do I have to take it if I don't want to
- How do I ace it
- Is it like the AP exam
- Is it similar to the ACT
- What score must I achieve to get into the college of my choice (SAT? ACT?)

So many questions and concerns hit you all at once. You look around and your classmates are feeling the same way. You need answers!

Well, we're please to supply them for you. Every year, we're hit with the same scenario: parents of anxious students contact us for help with a test. Some of which, feel it may be too late, but have no guidance.

We have compiled a checklist of "Five Easy and Awesome Steps to Prep"...

Step 1: Just Do It! – Get prep, that is!

Preparing for a test is essential to succeeding. Starting early can put you at an even better advantage. Even the simplest preparation is better than nothing at all. When you know how to pace yourself and understand what to expect on tests like the SAT, ACT, and PSAT, you're more likely to be prepared, confident and relaxed. This preparation reduces anxiety and stress, which leads to better scores. Getting preparation for any test can sometimes level the playing field for students.

According to a Huffington Post article on test prep, by virtue of simply taking one or more full-length practice exams under real test conditions in order to become more familiar with the test, students tend to improve their scores by 30 points. Studies have shown that students who prepare for these tests by focusing on areas of content where they have weaknesses and practicing test-taking strategies can improve their SAT scores anywhere from 100 to even 400 points, on average. Take a minute to view our quick SAT vs. ACT guide at the end of the chapter for a detailed comparison of the revised tests.

	SAT	**ACT**
Why Take It	Colleges use SAT scores for admissions and merit-based scholarships.	Colleges use ACT scores for admissions and merit-based scholarships.
Test Structure	• Math • Reading • Writing and Language • Essay (optional)	• Math • Reading • English • Science • Essay (optional)
Length	• 3 hours (without essay) • 3 hours, 50 minutes (with essay)	• 2 hours, 55 minutes (without essay) • 3 hours, 40 minutes (with essay)
Reading	Five (5) reading passages	Four (4) reading passages
Science	None	One (1) science section testing your critical thinking skills (not your specific science knowledge)
Math	Covers: • Arithmetic • Algebra I & II • Geometry, Trigonometry and Data Analysis	Covers: • Arithmetic • Algebra I & II • Geometry and Trigonometry
Tools	Some math questions don't allow you to use a calculator.	You can use a calculator on all math questions.
Essays	Optional. The essay will test your comprehension of a source text.	Optional. The essay will test how well you evaluate and analyze complex issues.
How It's Scored	Scored on a scale of 400–1600	Scored on a scale of 1–36

Step 2: Use your available resources

According to US News and World Report, students neglect to use available resources. Most teachers and high school counselors have resources that can help you. Sometimes students simply don't ask. Although some preparation services and programs may exceed your family's pocket, there are some very effective and affordable options.

Here are some helpful resources...

- Take a practice test: Most students are advised to take their first practice SAT or ACT test during their sophomore year of high school. Butterfly Works and Suited 4 Success College Planning Services partner throughout the year to offer Practice Test Days to students within the community. You can take a full-length ACT or SAT practice test in a classroom setting and get your scores back within a week. One added advantage to getting detailed score reports, along with the actual practice test booklet, is to see your areas of weakness and make a plan to achieve better scores through pacing and content study.

- Local community organizations and churches: Offer test preparation services within your community. Some Non-Profit Organizations offer educational services such as free SAT Prep course for youth within the community. There may be a church or organization close to your home or school that offers similar services. "Seek and ye shall find."

- Online resources: Take advantage of resources where they offer full College Board and ACT practice test questions and video explanations of some of the answers. Can you say helpful? (Be sure to check out our RESOURCES page)

- Fee Waivers: If you have financial restrictions – learning about the fee waiver process and how to acquire them for free/reduced lunch eligibility can be key to getting what you need. You may have access to College Application Fee Waivers, as well as ACT and SAT Fee Waivers/Vouchers.

- Super Scoring: another added benefit that students may forget to ask schools about. Some Universities and Colleges will use your highest section scores from all dates you've taken the test. So, you can use this when strategically taking multiple tests, by concentrating on one section of the test at a time. Research your college or university to inquire about Super Scoring.

- Test Optional Schools: Did you know that half of the Top 100 Liberal Arts Colleges don't require the SAT / ACT? According to **www.Fairtest.org**, (The National Center for Fair and Open Testing), a record number of colleges and universities now have test optional admissions policies. Some schools exempt students who meet minimum grade point average or class rank criteria; others require SAT or ACT scores but use them only for placement purposes. It's important that you contact your prospective school's admissions office for complete details.

- Study for the ACCUPLACER Test: Many students have the misconception that they don't need test prep when starting their education at a community college. This is simply not the case. You can prepare for this test to avoid taking costly courses in college, therefore shortening your time in school and reducing your bill. The ACCUPLACER test is not just for community colleges any more! Four-year colleges are starting to use this test for placement as well. It's a College Board administered test, so you can prepare for it.

- Put that smart phone to good use: In a recent Butterfly Works Scholar Think-Tank, students downloaded recommended apps and games to help with preparation.

Some of the top Apple / Google App Store picks...
  - Magoosh ACT Flashcards
  - SAT Up
  - Free Rice
  - Sheppard's Software
  - The Grading Game
  - ACT Math Jeopardy

You can use your phone for vocabulary help as well. Having an awesome vocabulary helps in so many ways. Using Instagram to view pictures of new vocabulary words can help visual learners. Downloading the **Dictionary.com** app is an amazing tool to strengthen vocabulary. When using the thesaurus portion of the app, you can identify synonyms of new words to connect context clues. Use cell phones to their full potential with your goal of becoming smarter.

Do your own comparison of the ACT and SAT Tests
Colleges accept both tests equally, so the choice is up to you! When students asks if they should take the ACT or the SAT, I

advise that they take them both – in practice test format first. The average SAT score is 1,000, which is about 500 in both sections. The SAT is graded on a scale of 200 – 800 in both Math and Evidence-Based Reading and Writing. The sections are combined to give a score of 400 – 1600. You'll earn one ACT score (1 to 36) on each test (English, Math, Reading and Science) and a composite ACT score, which is an average of these four tests. Usually, when people ask about your score, they're referring to your composite ACT score. The composite score falls between 1 and 36. The national average is about 21. For example, if you scored 31 on the English, 30 on the Math, 29 on the Reading and 30 on the Science, your composite ACT score would be 30. Both tests now have optional essay sections.

If you haven't taken either test, take the time to practice both of them to see which you prefer. The differences aren't that different anymore. Both tests still have their own subtle ways of testing different topics. For example, the ACT has a science section that deals more with analysis of data and experiments vs. how well you know chemistry. Although the SAT doesn't have a science section, it now has science-derived passages within its evidence-based reading and writing sections. Thus, it is important for you determine your own strengths and weaknesses before dedicating your time to just one particular test.

Step 3: Leave No Bubble Behind

This tip is definitely worth mentioning. Too often, I have scored practice tests and have shaken my head at students that leave too many of the questions blank. I so wish they had prepped. Unlike the previous SAT, the Redesigned version has NO Penalty. You get one (1) point for every question you get correct and NO POINTS for questions you get wrong or omit. Which means you can fill-in every bubble within a section after completing those you know. This is often called using your Letter of the Day (LOTD).

For example, when completing the math sections of the test, you don't have to do so in the order they are presented. You can immediately answer those that are easiest for you, while skipping those you don't know – TIME STEALERS. You can then go back and use Process of Elimination (POE) for those that are familiar to you. After you've done all that you can do correctly, implement your LOTD. Choose a letter: A, B, C or D and use it to fill in the blank bubbles you have left. You're bound to get a few extra points. This skill is also helpful on the ACT Test.

Step 4: Fifty Percent of Success is Showing Up – Prepared and Early

Parents often ask, "How may I assist my child throughout this process?" I am a strong advocate of parental support. The simplest things can mean so much. You can support by encouraging your child to stay sharp by using the SAT Question of the Day or the ACT Question of the Day phone apps. (Use that precious phone data for good). You can challenge them with new vocabulary from movies or commercials you watch. Create a special time for them to study, just a few minutes a day. That mental muscle will grow stronger over time.

Here's a cool list of things that can make test day even better...

- Provide your scholar with a healthy protein-rich breakfast

- Sleep: Ask them to "shut it down" before 10:30pm – they will look at you like you're crazy, but will love you in the morning. Remember you should arrive to your testing site by 7:45am

- Pack all of the following items on the night before the test
    - o Correct Calculator (Scientific or Graphing)
    - o Three Sharpened # 2 Pencils
    - o Water – because you need it.
    - o Snacks (good, high protein snacks you know they will like)
    - o A watch (so many discount this pace setting-helper; they may not have a clock in the testing room)
    - o A Sweater (just in case, as you never know the temperature of the rooms assigned
    - o Of course, you would want to map out directions to your testing site before test day

Step 5: Map your way to your target score

More often than not, students are not fully aware of easy ways to get the scores they want. Knowing how many questions to answer in each section can save you time, keep you focused and confident while working through questions. It's just like using Google Maps to show you the visual turns and distances to a particular place. With time and practice, you can even choose your shortest route. Preparing for a test can help you map your way to success. Knowing how many points to achieve within test sections can definitely help your confidence and reduce anxiety.

Here's a great scenario…

You research and discover that your college of choice accepted students with math scores between 570 – 610 last Fall. Your goal is to increase your score to a 590 after your first practice test. On the SAT, you are given 80 minutes to complete 58 questions. As part of your strategy, you find that you need to answer at least 34 questions correctly to get your desired score. Understanding that you still have a total of 80 minutes (with both math sections) to achieve that. Knowing your time and target number can be a game-changer. Don't forget you can still use your LOTD!

Top 5 Most Frequently Asked Questions from Parents...

- **Should the essays be completed for both exams?**

    Answer: It varies, but I recommend doing the essay if you are not sure of your college choices. College Board has a convenient list of schools and their essay policies to determine if your school prefers it be taken or not.

- **How many times should students plan to take either test to feel comfortable with the format and increase their chances of doing well?**

    Answer: At least twice, with preparation and a practice test in-between. If a student starts in their sophomore year, they should take a practice test first to identify their weaknesses "off the record". Students traditionally take the official SAT and ACT in the winter and spring of their junior year and, if necessary, again in the fall of their senior year. This gives them more flexibility to decide which test would be the best retake – the SAT or ACT tests one or more times.

Some important questions you should ask yourself when planning your test-taking schedule...

- What are my deadlines for college and scholarships
- How many times do I want to take the SAT/ACT

- Am I trying to improve my scores in all sections with each retake or using a "super-scoring" strategy
- How long do I plan to study

- **How do SAT scores make up for moderate to low GPA's?**

  Answer: There are cases where scores and GPA are seen on a sliding scale to balance the two. For student athletes, the NCAA Clearinghouse uses a sliding scale for this purpose. If you have a low-test score, you will need a higher GPA to be eligible and if you have a low GPA, they require you to have a higher test score. Go to **www.ncaa.org** for details.

- **With so much that is required of my child during the school year, when is the best time to enroll my child in a test prep program (summer, holidays, spring break)?**

  Answer: At Butterfly Works, we are true fans of summer and winter break. We have sessions of "Prep While No One's Looking", where we encourage students to take their downtime and put it to good use. During the summer, one can concentrate on concepts a little easier without compounding homework and schoolwork. It's a great time to improve and focus on a particular area of need, as well.

- **What are SAT Subject Tests and should my student take one?**

  Answer: SAT Subject Tests are separate tests taken to highlight your scholar's ability in a particular subject. There are five subject areas: Math, Science, English,

History and Languages. Some schools will request that a student take the SAT Subject Test, especially if your student is interested in areas like technology, economics, engineering or science. Remember, they are not to be mistaken for the SAT Reasoning Test, which is generally requested of all applicants.

Although the vocabulary-focused sentence completion section was removed from the SAT, we still encourage scholars to continue strengthening their lexicon. It is imperative that students recognize key words and be able to use context clues featured within the new evidence-based reading and writing sections. Here is a head start in the process of building an awesome vocabulary.

Top 15 most commonly used words on the SAT...

- Acerbic – sour or bitter in taste

- Anomalous – unusual, abnormal

- Austere – strict, simple, harsh, or frugal

- Candid – straightforward, natural, sincere

- Dire – serious, urgent, or terrible

- Egregious – shockingly bad, atrocious

- Malleable – easily influenced, soft enough to be shaped

- Nonchalant – cool as a cucumber

- Nuance – subtle differences or context

- Obsequious – excessively obedient, submissive (a person who is a "doormat")

- Obsolete – out of date (think flip phones and cassette tapes)
- Paradoxical – seemingly opposite (huge universe is made of tiny atoms)
- Petulant – childishly pouting
- Stark – total, severe (often used in the phrase "stark contrast")
- Unmitigated – downright, total, utter (usually negative)

Top 15 most commonly used words on the ACT...

- Analyze – examine in detail
- Compose – write or create, constitute, make up
- Correlate – have a mutual relationship or connection
- Critical – expressing adverse or disapproving comments or judgments
- Determine – cause something to occur in a particular way
- Differentiate – recognize or ascertain what makes
- Engage – occupy, attract, or involve
- Emerge – become apparent, important, or prominent
- Evolve – develop gradually, especially from a simple to a more complex form
- Infer – deduce or conclude information from evidence and reasoning rather than from explicit statements
- Omit – leave out or exclude someone or something

- Precede – come before something in time
- Redundant – not or no longer needed or useful
- Reflect – of a surface or body throw back heat, light, or sound
- Relevant – closely connected or appropriate to the matter at hand

Butterfly WORKS

Shuyinthia T. Farley-Hembry, CEO, Chief Academic Officer of *Butterfly Works, LLC* has dedicated her time and resources to supporting people of all walks of life, but feels most passionate to work with those who desire to increase their academic opportunities. Since May 2000, "Ms. Shuy", (as her students affectionately call her) has worked as a private academic tutor. Mrs. Shuyinthia Hembry is a native Washingtonian and has attended local schools, graduating from Duke Ellington School for the Arts. She studied Psychology and Music at the George Washington University. Mrs. Hembry is an accomplished violinist, loves calligraphy, jazz and golf. Shuyinthia is married to Kevin Hembry, the love of her life.

Butterfly Works was birthed in June 2006, *to inspire students to succeed in every educational arena and life through personalized academic enrichment services to individuals and small groups.* *Butterfly Works,* helps students achieve higher grades and increase standardized test scores in the following areas: PSAT, SAT, ACT, HSPT, SSAT, and ISEE. *Butterfly Works,* helps students master skills in specific academic subjects, college entry tests and career tests. Our academic services include tutoring in: Math, English, Social Studies, History, Science and Writing. We pair scholars with tutors who are subject-matter experts to increase our students' academic successes. Students enjoy our creative approach to education and families note the marked improvement in their student's confidence, test scores and grades.

Additionally, *Butterfly Works* offers Financial Literacy Workshops that allow students the opportunity to learn important "real world" economic concepts while having fun. We use creative games, virtual economic platforms, and hypothetical stock market investments in online portfolios. These resources introduce approaches to money that the students will use for the rest of their lives, giving them an added social advantage in the real world.

In 2015, *Butterfly Works* expanded their partnership within the community to offer SAT Prep classes in several classrooms within the District of Columbia's Public and Charter Schools. Shuyinthia believes that, "Students' minds are like butterflies, they never go back to caterpillars after learning to fly."

Butterfly Works has enjoyed many years of philanthropy, as we've served students, increased partnerships, participated in College Tours, established an annual graphing calculator drive, and given numerous college scholarships. We love our community and embrace the brilliance of our youth.

"Transforming Minds to ELEVATE!"
Shuyinthia Farley-Hembry
CEO, Academic Chief Officer
Butterfly Works, LLC

Strategic Move 4

Crafting Your Unique Story

It's essay time!!! I can hear the screech of your scream and the immediate conversation you are having in your head as you say...

- I am not a good writer
- Why can't I just interview
- I don't know what to write about
- 650 words that's way too much
- What is a personal statement
- How do I know if the reader will like my story

These are all valid concerns, but before you break into a frenzy let me share some ways you can overcome your fears and write a stellar essay.

First let me take a moment to be very transparent with you. I had all the same concerns when writing my college essay as you; I was not an avid writer. No one told me it was acceptable to write from a creative standpoint as long as you used proper grammatical writing. Once I got over my fear, I wrote an ok college essay. At least I believe so since I got into college. Imagine if I knew then what I know today I would have written a stellar essay. Enough about me. I am going to share insight with you about crafting your unique stellar essay. While it may not be the most exciting part of the application process, remember it helps an admissions committee decide whether or not you are ideal for their program. Are you ready? I'm sure you answered yes, so lets jump right in.

When Should You Write Your Personal Essay? The spring of your junior year is a great time to work on your personal essay. If you feel that's too soon at the very least, I would recommend starting two to three months before your deadlines. I'm sure none of you have ever stayed up all night writing an essay due the next day, or maybe you have.

There are five types of essay writers…

- Started Three Weeks Ago
- Did It Last Night
- Did It This Morning
- Still Working On It
- Just Straight Up Forgot

This is one essay you shouldn't leave for a last minute all-nighter. Put the time and thought into crafting an essay that admissions officers will remember. Most students struggle with honing in on a specific experience that reveals something unique and significant about their identity in a few words (650 to be exact) for the common application. The Common Application prompts are designed to elicit information that will strengthen the other components of the application.

Scott Anderson, former school counselor and current Senior Director for Programs and Partnerships for The Common Application says, "We want to make sure that every applicant can find a home within the essay prompts, and that they can use the prompts as a starting point to write an essay that is authentic and distinguishing." Among the more than 800,000 unique applicants who submitted a Common App during the 2015-2016 application cycle, 47 percent chose to write about their background, identity, interest, or talent - making it the most frequently selected prompt; 22 percent chose to write about an accomplishment, 17 percent about a lesson or failure, 10 percent about a problem solved, and four percent about an idea challenged. "With the 2017-2018 application fast approaching the common application has made revisions to their questions in order to help all applicants, regardless of background or access to counseling, see themselves and their stories within the prompts. They are designed to invite unencumbered discussions of character and community, identity, and aspiration." For more information visit the **www.commonapp.org.**

What question will you choose?

- Some students have a background, identity, interest, or talent that is so meaningful they believe their application would be incomplete without it. If this sounds like you, then please share your story.

- The lessons we take from *obstacles we encounter* can be fundamental to later success. Recount a time when you faced a *challenge, setback, or failure.* How did it affect you, and what did you learn from the experience?

- Reflect on a time when you *questioned* or challenged a belief or idea. What prompted your *thinking*? What was the *outcome*?

- Describe a problem you've solved or a problem you'd like to solve. It can be an intellectual challenge, a research query, an ethical dilemma - anything that is of personal importance, no matter the scale. Explain its significance to you and what steps you took or could be taken to identify a solution.

- Discuss an accomplishment, event, or *realization* that *sparked a period of personal growth and a new understanding of yourself or others.*

- Describe a topic, idea, or concept you find so engaging that it makes you lose all track of time. Why does it captivate you? What or who do you turn to when you want to learn more?

- Share an essay on any topic of your choice. It can be one you've already written, one that responds to a different prompt, or one of your own design.

When writing keep in mind these two important things...

- Your essay should provide evidence of your achievements that are not reflected in other areas of your application
- "How" and "Why" the _____ you described shaped your attitude, focus, and, intellectual vitality

The foundation to writing and revising a winning stellar college essay is allowing your unique voice to be heard by...

- **Making your Introduction go Boom!**
  Ensure your introduction paragraph opens with a bang. You could quickly lose your audience if you fail to do this. Remember this is the first thing the reader will lay eyes on. This is your opportunity to capture the admissions committee's attention. Don't give away the story, intrigue the reader and leave them wanting more.

- **Engaging your Audience**
  The personal statement provides you with an opportunity to shine the lights on your unique experiences and talents. Share your story in a compelling way, do not just list facts and make general statements. Paint a vivid and colorful picture for the reader. Remember they don't know your story, you do. Remember first impressions are lasting impressions. Make an impactful one by creating a story that will come alive.

- **Spotlighting the Specifics**
  Ensure you provide specific examples in demonstrating both the "how" and "why" behind your topic through concrete examples. Be sure to clearly explain to the reader(s) how you plan to achieve your goals and why you chose them in the first place. If you aspire to become an engineer, explain how you plan to arrive at that profession as well as the experiences that led you to pursue your dream. The stronger you convey your purpose, the more you will stand out among the many essays the committee will read.

- **Unveiling the Hidden Treasures about each Institution**
  When applying to an academic program, it is important to convey why you are pursuing this particular program and university over others. Be sure to talk a little about the history and opportunities the school can offer you, as well as what makes it unique. This will demonstrate to the admissions committee that you have done your research in determining if their school is the right fit. When outlining how you would benefit from the program, remember to communicate what you can contribute to the program.

- **Revising, Proof-reading, Revising and Proof-reading**
  Proofread until your essay is done. Although proofreading and revising can be tedious and time-consuming you can never have too many drafts. Remember two sets of eyes are always better than one. Be sure to have a family member, instructor or mentor review your essay for comments and feedback. Last minute produces sloppy work. Even an essay with a compelling story can end up in the "no" pile if basic grammar and writing skills are ignored.

A Compelling Essay ...

Exemplifies a creative and unique story that...

- Provides the reader with a vivid and compelling picture of you
- Focuses on your achievements, goals, and values
- Captures the reader's attention in the introduction by getting right to the point using precise language and vivid imagery

Exemplifies quality not quantity...

- Quality counts
- A good essay is not a list of your accomplishments
- Demonstrates knowledge of the major/school

Reveal best practices in writing...

- Utilization of proper grammar, sentence structure and word usage
- Feedback from others helps to identify areas of your essay that work well and those that don't
- Remember to check your spelling Microsoft word is not a dictionary

Follow guidelines...

- Follow the guidelines for word count
- Be sure to examine and answer the question being asked
- Remember less is not more and more does not mean quality

Exemplifies confidence as you end with fireworks...

- A good essay doesn't beg or brag
- Exude quiet confidence as you reveal yourself through

your description of lifelong interests, sustained commitment, and/or perseverance in the face of adversity

- The reader does not want to hear complaints about poor grades or bad circumstances, instead they want to know how you overcame them

A Compelling Essay Will Not...

- Repeat information contained elsewhere in the application

- Complain about life's circumstances and not explain them

- Discuss cost or ranking as a contributing factor in applying to a particular major/college

- Provide fluff over substance

- Provide information that is not backed up in their application

- Reference the wrong school name

- Contain grammatical errors, sentence structure errors, clichés or meaningless usage

- Meet or exceed the requirements

The essay is an integral part of the application process it serves as your opportunity to shine the spotlight on you and give the reader a feel for you as a person as well as a student. So let's get started. The first stage of writing is brainstorming. It is the process of gathering all your ideas and recording them on paper without making edits or changes. I know you are saying shouldn't I always make sure to spell and use correct English when writing? Of course, however not during brainstorming. You can think more creative when you're not restricted by rules. This is a time to allow all your creative juices to flow on to the paper.

It's time to gather and organize your information...

Step 1: Read over your writing without making any changes this time .

Step 2: Go back and read through again with your favorite color highlighter and mark the ideas, thoughts, and points you feel are important.

Step 3: Begin to group similar ideas on a separate sheet of paper.

Step 4: Now read through all your notes and identify one idea you feel will allow your unique voice to resound from the page in a unique way.

Here are some key areas you most likely uncovered ...

- An achievement that you're proud of
- An event or experience that taught you a lesson
- The strength or courage of someone who has made an impact in your life
- An experience that influenced you in some way
- An event that defines your background

Now that you have pages of ideas, thoughts, strengths, weaknesses, and highlights begin, but don't forget the rules of writing.

An essay consist of the following...

Introduction (3-5 sentences): purpose is to present your position known as the thesis or argument – a clear, one-sentence explanation of your position that leaves no doubt in the reader's mind about which side you are on from the beginning of your essay.

Note: In your college essay the introduction carries more meaning. It is a place for you to "hook" the attention of your audience – you make them want to continue reading.

Body Paragraph's I, II, & III (5-10 sentences): collectively known to spell out in detail the examples that support your thesis. Each paragraph's first sentence should be the topic sentence of the paragraph.

Note: The first body paragraph should convey your strongest argument or most significant point by explaining to the reader, in detail, who or what an example is and, more importantly, why that example is relevant. The remaining body paragraphs should follow the same direction.

Conclusion (3-5 sentences): is not an afterthought. It holds just as much value as it represents your last chance to summarize and back up your points.

Note: You should end your conclusion with fireworks it's your last chance to make a final impression.

Now it is time to begin writing your stellar essay. Be sure to address the following questions in your essay...

- What were the key moments and details during the _____
- What did I learn from this _____
- What aspect of the _____ stays with me most
- What does this _____ reveal about me
- What makes the _____ special or significant
- How does this _____ make me special or make me stand out
- What truth about me is revealed through this _____

Writing can be a challenge and it is very important in the college application process. Begin thinking about it early. You will go through several changes in topics before discovering the best one. Remember to express yourself as clearly, powerfully, and vividly as you can. Don't be afraid to gain feedback from friends, parents, and teachers and incorporate their suggestions in your essay. Proofread and double check everything before pressing submit. In the end, it's your voice and your story to tell.

"Mind Map to a Stellar Essay"

By now you're saying what is a Mind Map? I thought you would never ask. It is one of my favorite things to do. In fact I map out everything even writing down everything needed from start to finish in writing this book. When you take time to map out everything needed to accomplish something it helps to eliminate what we call "BRAIN FREEZE."

I'm sure you're asking how will this help me write a stellar essay? Creating a Mind Map to plan your essay, you generate more ideas quickly and, you can quickly see the connecting topics, main paragraphs and structure. It helps you to make a realistic plan for your essay, and create a logical structure for the introduction, main sections and conclusions.

Here's how it goes...

Step 1: Inner Circle is where you jot down your main topic
Step 2: Outer circles are so you can write out key areas that support your main topic
Step 3: Now you take the middle circle and create a sentence that sets the foundation for your paragraph
Step 4: Then you take the subsequent outer circles and create supporting sentences for every key area you identified that supports the foundation you created in your main sentence

If you follow this structure it will help to keep your mind focused on your core message and eliminate the chance of you going off track and doing the unthinkable "rambling". A Mind Map triggers your brain to take a thought and instantly spark creative ideas that will lead you to one thing "your unique story".

Introduction – Mind Map

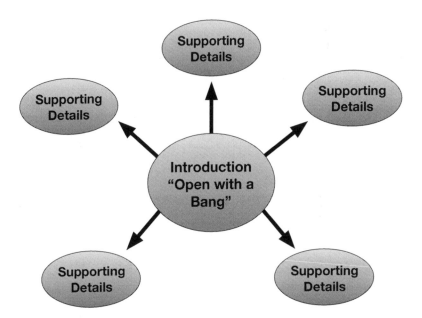

Body Paragraph 1 – Mind Map

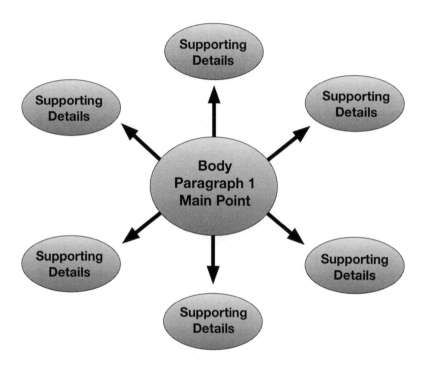

Body Paragraph 2 – Mind Map

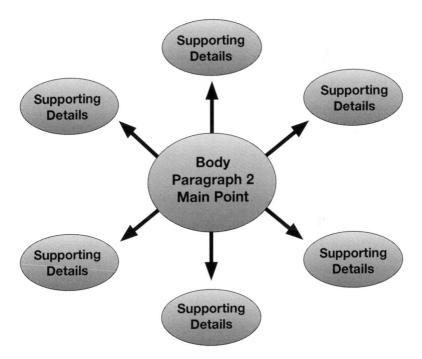

Body Paragraph 3 – Mind Map

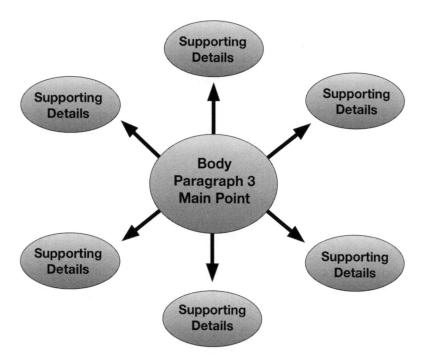

Conclusion – Mind Map

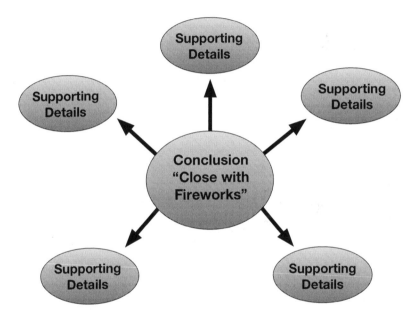

Testimonials

The Suited 4 Success Program has been a blessing. Ms. Robinson has been AWESOME throughout the college application process and I don't know how I would have made it through without her. It started with the college tour which helped expose me to colleges that I otherwise would not have seen. The help provided with my college essays, the application process and meeting deadlines was right on point. My mom went out of town for a period of time during application filing and Ms. Robinson never let me miss a beat. Thank you Suited 4 Success for all your help!!

-Myles Anderson, Riverdale Baptist High School, Class of 2019

Suited 4 Success really helped with me with the college application process. I received monthly scholarships to fill out, help with my essays and submitted all my applications ahead of time. MS. Regina gave me great advice and guidance along the way. Before S4S, I was thinking how could I navigate the college admission process. I didn't know where to begin and what first steps to take until I met Ms. Regina. With Ms.Regina's support and guidance, I got accepted into all five of my colleges with scholarship money!

-Ebony Brockman, Charles Herbert Flowers High School, Class of 2019

Parents have been raving about how Winning The Game Of College Admissions was a #1 resource for helping their high school students prepare for the college admissions process!

Grab your copy
http://bit.ly/WinningTheGame

"College Essay Samples"

Sample Essay 1

Stinson graciously shared her Common Application admissions essay with Business Insider, which we've reprinted verbatim below.

Prompt 1: Some students have a background, identity, interest, or talent that is so meaningful they believe their application would be incomplete without it. If this sounds like you, then please share your story.

Managing to break free from my mother's grasp, I charged. With arms flailing and chubby legs fluttering beneath me, I was the ferocious two¬ year old rampaging through Costco on a Saturday morning. My mother's eyes widened in horror as I jettisoned my churro; the cinnamon sugar rocket gracefully sliced its way through the air while I continued my spree. I sprinted through the aisles, looking up in awe at the massive bulk products that towered over me. Overcome with wonder, I wanted to touch and taste, to stick my head into industrialized freezers, to explore every crevice. I was a conquistador, but rather than searching the land for El Dorado, I scoured aisles for free samples. Before inevitably being whisked away into a shopping cart, I scaled a mountain of plush toys and surveyed the expanse that lay before me: the kingdom of Costco.

Notorious for its oversized portions and dollar fifty hot dog combo, Costco is the apex of consumerism. From the days spent being toted around in a shopping cart to when I was finally tall enough to reach lofty sample trays, Costco has endured a steady presence throughout my life. As a veteran Costco shopper, I navigate the aisles of foodstuffs, thrusting the majority of my weight upon a generously filled shopping cart whose enormity juxtaposes my small frame. Over time, I've developed a habit of observing fellow patrons tote their carts piled with frozen burritos, cheese puffs, tubs of ice cream, and weight loss supplements. Perusing the aisles gave me time to ponder. Who needs three pounds of sour cream? Was cultured yogurt any more well-mannered than its uncultured counterpart? Costco gave birth to my unfettered curiosity.

While enjoying an obligatory hot dog, I did not find myself thinking about the 'all beef' goodness that Costco boasted. I instead considered finitudes and infinitudes, unimagined uses for tubs of sour cream, the projectile motion of said tub when launched from an eighty foot shelf or maybe when pushed from a speedy cart by a scrawny seventeen year old. I contemplated the philosophical: If there exists a thirty-three ounce jar of Nutella, do we really have free will? I experienced a harsh physics lesson while observing a shopper who had no evident familiarity of inertia's workings. With a cart filled to overflowing, she made her way towards the sloped exit, continuing to push and push while steadily losing control until the cart escaped her and went crashing into a concrete column, 52" plasma screen TV and all. Purchasing the yuletide hickory smoked ham inevitably led to a conversation between my father and me about Andrew Jackson's controversiality. There was no questioning Old Hickory's dedication; he was steadfast in his beliefs and pursuits – qualities I am compelled to admire, yet his morals were crooked. We both found the ham to be more likeable–and tender.

I adopted my exploratory skills, fine-tuned by Costco, towards my intellectual endeavors. Just as I sampled buffalo chicken dip or chocolate truffles, I probed the realms of history, dance and biology, all in pursuit of the ideal cart–one overflowing with theoretical situations and notions both silly and serious. I sampled calculus, cross country running, scientific research, all of which are now household favorites. With cart in hand, I do what scares me; I absorb the warehouse that is the world. Whether it be through attempting aerial yoga, learning how to chart black-body radiation using astronomical software, or dancing in front of hundreds of people, I am compelled to try any activity that interests me in the slightest.

My intense desire to know, to explore beyond the bounds of rational thought; this is what defines me. Costco fuels my insatiability and cultivates curiosity within me at a cellular level. Encoded to immerse myself in the unknown, I find it difficult to complacently accept the "what"; I want to hunt for the "whys" and dissect the "hows". In essence, I subsist on discovery.

http://www.businessinsider.com/high-school-senior-who-got-into-5-ivy-league-schools-shares-her-admissions-essay-2016-4

Sample Essay 2

What motivates you to do it? Do you know the reason why? You are carrying out that very simple action at this moment, because it is extremely vital. Most of us forget that we are doing it, we call it breathing; which is difficult for some but easy for others. It surprises me that we never give breathing significant conscious thought. With every breath I take; my aspirations and thoughts of pursuing my passion to dance, understand different cultures and study science come alive. When I dance I feel empowered, each breath gives me strength to become the woman God has destined for me to be. Dance has become a therapeutic way for me to clear my mind, organize my thoughts, and desires. The pressure of every day life can sometimes be overwhelming so when I feel the pressure I take time to relax and breathe. With every breath comes a new idea, perspective and desire to gain knowledge in my efforts to become a well-rounded student.

As a young woman, I am intrigued by the many different cultures; issues and perspectives women are facing around the world. In 2013, I was given the opportunity to travel to Rwanda. While there I witnessed the importance of cultural awareness, change in government, and the collective effort necessary to bring a country back from such a devastating time. I was extremely proud of the newly empowered women of Rwanda. "Currently, sixty four percent of the seats in Rwanda's parliament are held by women, this is more than any other country in the world". Although Rwanda has made huge strides there is still more work to be done in their public health system. For years, it has been my passion to pursue a career in the medical field. Visiting Rwanda was an epiphany for me because instantly I realized my true passion is to become a doctor and study international medicine. My goal is to travel the world and help improve the lives of people in developing countries by providing them with adequate medical care. Providing medical care to individuals and building the capacity for sustainable health care systems in developing countries is something that I know with every breath I get closer to achieving. As I continue to remind myself to never take life for granted, strive for the best and acknowledge that with every breath there is the beginning of something new and a chance to make an impact on the world.

Sample Essay 3

Coco Chanel states: "Fashion is not something that exists in dresses only. Fashion is in the sky, in the street; fashion has to do with ideas, the way we live, what is happening." Growing up near Washington, DC which is one of the fashion capitols in the United States after New York City is intriguing. My many visits to New York City have inspired my true love for the many facets fashion offers. I enjoy expressing myself through the art of fashion as I explore the different styles, trends and cultures. Growing up I always wanted to become a fashion designer; I would put on fashion shows for my friends and family right in my living room. I would look through magazines and newspapers cutting out pictures of the latest fashion trends and styles. I knew becoming a fashion designer was exactly what I wanted to do, until in 6th grade I discovered fashion was just one of many pieces to the puzzle. I realized while doing a creative writing piece on fashion that writing was my true passion.

I began putting all my time into writing stories and reading articles. As social media continues to evolve; I created my very own blog as my first open line of communication with the world. In my quest to find what I want to do in life I realized I could combine my passion for fashion and writing as a journalist. As I prepare for the next phase of my journey as a fashion journalist, I am motivated to bring awareness to the very presence fashion plays in everyday life. Attending Howard University will grant me the foundation needed to enhance my knowledge and insight in the field of Journalism and Mass Communication. The many facets offered within the Journalism program at Howard University; writing, audio recording, editing and videotaping, video production and editing skills will allow me to graduate as a well-rounded Journalist. The history of Historically Black Colleges and Universities has paved the way for African American students to journey in the footsteps of those who came before them. I am intrigued by the accomplishments of the many successful alumni Journalist who have come before me and paved the way. Researching and reading the success stories of alumni who studied in the school of Journalism and Mass Communications program from Howard University, encourages me that I am making the right choice in choosing Howard to pursue my post-secondary education. Following in the footsteps of my mother as a Howard University graduate encourages me to continue the legacy. The culture, history, beauty, and significance that Howard University exemplifies excite me in my efforts to become a part of the history as I strive to achieve my educational and career goals. I know it is necessary to embrace my education as I continue to mature and blossom into a well-rounded student, woman and journalist. I believe my drive, poise and determination to succeed makes me a great addition to the Bison family.

Sample Essay 4

The memories that come along with attending high school are usually very influential to a person's life. These are the years when you make the friends of a lifetime, share new experiences, and begin to find out who you're really supposed to be. In the beginning of my sophomore year, I began attending one of the most prestigious private high schools in Maryland, The Bullis School. I was so apprehensive about starting a new school because I would be placed outside of my comfort zone.

My first day was horrid; I felt as though I was a small fish within a vast ocean. The combination of being rushed through crowded halls, not knowing where any of my classes were, and feeling secluded in the lunch room, brought upon a feeling of disdain for my new found school. As a new student I felt alone and out of place; it was as if everyone had good friends except for me. But little did I know this was all about to change. The most unlikely place was going to become where I felt most comfortable.

Over the loud speaker I heard an announcement for all girls to report to the auditorium, there was a mandatory girls meeting. As all the girls in the high school depicted their life stories, I suddenly felt a change of heart. As I looked at all the girl's faces I realized I didn't know them. It was rude of me to dislike them just because I was a new student. So that day, I decided to make a 100% effort to get to know as many people as possible. As months passed I transformed into a social butterfly. I had bonded with a set group of girls, but I also socialized with everyone else; attending sports games, birthday parties, and sleepovers. Students began approaching me for advice or just to vent. I was a friend to everyone, and everyone was a friend to me. I also became close to many of my teachers. I made a good impression by joining a myriad of clubs, participating in class discussions, and upholding academic excellence. Sometimes we even ate lunch together and got to know one another on a personal level. Every day I could walk into school always be myself, if I had anything on my chest there was always someone there to listen. The people in the school embraced me and made me feel as if I was a part of an extended family.

I no longer attend this school anymore but still to this day the teachers and students remember me. My friends and I still keep in touch; I still attend games and parties and the teachers still contact my mother to check up on me. This school became an environment where I was perfectly content; it means so much to me because I started off loathing it but in the end my perspective changed and I absolutely loved it.

Sample Essay 5

Munakata Reisi once uttered these words: "Family is the soci-ety that you came into contact with first; the people who influ-ence you first. But if that first society abandons you, there will be another society to accept you." This quote describes the coerce environment of my household as my parents are surely pushing me away. As an introvert, I am forced to find consolation in an environment I never imagined.

It is senior year and I refuse to continue looking like an awk-ward freshman. Clutching my bag, I made my way out the door, rammed into another student and knocked over almost all her belongings. The outraged girl spouted curses like they were a whole new language. I muttered, "I'm so sorry," repeatedly as I bent down to pick up her books. As I gathered her things, I accidentally knocked her phone out of her hand; imagine her language this time. I picked up her phone, mumbled one last apology and bolted to first period. I felt so embarrassed and I had no friends to talk to. Then, as if my conscious sent a telepathic wave to the other side of the planet, my phone received a Twitter notification.

"Hey, how are you?" It was Arran, an Australian who shared a lot of similarities with me. I told him about the incident that occurred and he responded, "OMG she seems kind of mean. Just run if you ever see her again lol." He continued, "Drop your phone and fly to Argentina, and I'm sure you'll be fine." I responded with several laughing emoticons before I received another notifi-cation. This time it was Kimmie. "Curse her out, girl! Who she think she talking to?" I chuckled and responded, "No, I'm not like that." Despite having an opposite personality from me, I look up to Kimmie as she has given me heartfelt advice and self-assur-ance that I've never received anywhere else.

The bell rang indicating class had started so I bid my friends goodbye. The day went by like a three-toed sloth; I mentally shouted, "Why is it still Tuesday?" When the final bell rang, I found my bus as quickly as possible. I entered the house, discarded my clothing, and lunged to the comfort of my bed. Before I realized I had fallen asleep, my mother burst through the door. In her typically loud voice she commanded, "Get out of bed and do your homework." I retaliated, "It's the first day of school; I have no homework. Can't I sleep?" She replied, "You can find something to do. You have to work and make sacrifices..." I had heard this speech a hundred times during summer vacation. While everyone was having fun, I was doing work. God forbid I take one day to relax. Since I had no homework, I vented on Twitter about what happened with my mother. I got no reply, but that's the beauty of Twitter; I tweet as if I have no followers at all.

Since no one replied, I found myself on YouTube watching random videos. One was a man complaining that social media belittled individuals and kept them from meeting new people. He stated how it narrows the perspective of the mind and prevents people from making friends. Of course it's not the same as meeting someone in real life, but the relationships I've developed online are much more meaningful than the "friendships" I've made face-to-face. Through Twitter, I have met people around the globe so similar to me, yet so different. From boldfaced "older sister" Kimmie and "big brother" Jay to socially anxious Arran and Norwegian athlete Joa, I have formed a family-like bond with my followers. My "unofficial family" fills my mentions with worried messages, sincere advice, and witty jokes. They have been there for me when my actual family couldn't be, and I have no regrets. It feels good to have friends.

Sample Essay 6

The Curtain rises. There I stand in a puddle of sweat, panting for dear life. My body is so overheated; I feel as if I might faint. These jelly arms of mine are wearing thin; my abs are trembling from the pain; my head has the sound of a personal drummer pounding away at my skull; will I make it? "Forty down, thirty-five more to go"; these pushups are torture, yet I know the benefits I will reap are worth the sweat and tears. I keep telling myself, "Push through it"; despite my fatigue I finish. I sit there as my body recuperates from the exhausting exercise.

Fast-forward a couple of months later. Standing backstage, me and my cast mates pray before taking the stage in hopes that all goes well. As the lights fade we move to our places. Butterflies fill my stomach as I anxiously listen to our MC introduce us. When the music starts and the lights come up; I put a smile on my face and hit the stage. The crowd loves every moment of the performance, their excitement motivating us to perform at our best. Two hours later, the show is over and it is time for curtain call; the crowd gives a standing ovation; as we stand and watch with gigantic smiles on our faces.

It all started my freshman year of school when my childhood best friend asked me to audition with her. Unfortunately, she did not make the cast, but I did and I decided to continue what we started. Walking into practice the first day, I was anxious because I was one of only four freshmen to join the cast of veterans that were already great friends. My nervousness quickly subsided when those same veterans, who were older and more intimidating, welcomed me with open arms and became some of my closest friends. After the warm welcome, I relaxed and realized that I was in the place I needed to be. When the workouts were challenging, I always had someone to help me keep going. When I did not understand the choreography, someone always retaught it to me; or when I was down and exhausted, someone was always there to make me laugh or feel better.

It may appear as though I am only a part of my school's drama club for the applause, friends and compliments, but that is not the case. In my school's auditorium, with my fellow Jaguar Players, is where I am home. During the whole eight-month period; from practices to the shows—I am with my chosen family. Not only are my cast mates a part of my new family, but also the adults that created our shows: my teacher, the choreographer, the music director, the makeup artist, the costume designer, and the technical director. They all became like aunts and uncles, making sure we developed our craft superbly for our shows.

In addition to the love, care, and support of those around me, being a part of the Jaguar Players for almost four years has given me a chance to grow and mature as a person. Today, I play the role that my fellow cast mates played for me when I first started: friend, motivator, and teacher. This year I have been given the opportunity to assist the choreographer. This allows me to use my creativity and skills I have developed over the years and give back, in a different way, to the club I love so much. Being on stage with my fellow Jaguar Players is where I am content because it is truly a place where I can be myself and mature into a young lady while being surrounded by loved ones.

Sample Essay 7

When entering high school, I had my four years all planned out. I was going to attend all the football games, party like a normal teenager, maintain academic success, and pursue my modeling dreams. I entered my school excited about what freshmen year would bring; new friends, fun, excitement, and of course the anxiety of high school. My excitement quickly faded away when I began to have "outer body experiences". Instead of doing the normal things freshmen do, I spent countless hours reading and researching, hoping to find solutions to my fading health. My life changed in the blink of an eye; I was forced to grow up all too quickly.

Can you imagine bending over the toilet doing your usual throwing up, but this time not remembering what happened? Well that was me, throwing up had become regular; but passing out took reality to a level of fear that was indescribable. That day I went from having a great time to being thrown into hospital beds all throughout the Washington, D.C area for multiple tests. No one could provide my family with concrete answers, just speculations. It was not until one day I had a Grand Mal seizure at home, that the doctors were able to shed light on my illness. That day I learned for the first time what the term Epilepsy really meant.

I began to fear my disease in fact smudge my entire high school journey. Could everything I knew to be normal change; my grades, my ability to pursue my dreams, and most importantly, my freedom? Instantly I went from being a teenager without responsibilities to one who was responsible for taking daily anti-seizure and headache medication in order to control my health. With the uncertainty of what medications worked best, I was forced to miss a lot of school. However, this did not deter me;

I worked hard to complete all my assignments and received extra assistance when needed from my teachers. When I returned to school I wondered if everyone knowing about my seizures would begin to cost me friendships or expose what I felt were my imperfections. Or maybe bring my community of friends even closer. To my surprise everyone at school showered me with support, open arms and love.

Still feeling like an outcast, despite all the support; my mother gave me a book to read over the summer of my junior year; "The Game of Life and How to Play it," by Florence Scovel Shinn. After reading the book my entire perspective about my disease changed. One thing that resonated with me was Ms. Shinn's positive affirmations and teachings about overcoming doubt and fear. Three years ago, I was fearful of the numerous EEG's, blood test, and extended sleep exams and wires hooked up to my head. What I viewed as a medical nightmare, I now view as my testimony. My endless fears, cries and worries are now a true testament to my confidence as a young woman determined to embrace my journey.

Although, I still have epilepsy, my seizures are now controlled and I can finally be a normal, crazy senior. The last four years has brought out the best in me; I believe if you pray and have faith, anything is possible. My recovery has allowed me to realize that God is a true healer. I am forever grateful to my doctors, teachers, family, and God for helping me through my ordeal. I am a proud to share my story and empower other young children and teens that suffer from Epilepsy; "to remain strong, gain knowledge and never give up the fight". Today, I am proud of the young woman I have become and no matter what life throws my way, giving up is not an option!

Strategic Move 5

Financing Your Education

If completing the Free Application for Federal Student Aid (FAFSA) is intimidating to your family, don't worry you're not alone. Most families worry about how they will finance their students' education. Realizing that paying for college is one of the largest expenses the family will incur. It is no secret that every family wants their student to receive a full ride scholarship or some form of financial aid to assist with paying for college. Completing the FAFSA is one of the main factors in colleges and universities determining a student's eligibility for federal student aid. It is used to apply for financial aid from the federal and state government and most colleges and universities.

Should Students Fill Out Both the FAFSA and CSS Profile? Yes, the FAFSA awards families with federal grants, scholarships and student loans while the CSS helps schools award non-federal institutional aid. The CSS PROFILE does not take the place of the FAFSA; rather it is an additional application for nonfederal financial aid as a supplement to the FAFSA by over 250 private colleges and universities for awarding funds. Unlike the FAFSA, there is a fee to apply. The first application is $25.00 and reports to additional schools are $16.00 each, fee waivers to cover the cost are granted to high-need students. The CSS application can be filed as early as October 1st, but no later than two weeks before the college's priority admission application deadline. However, the application should be completed as soon as possible in order to take advantage of aid that is distributed on a first-come, first-served basis. Schools requiring the CSS profile generally meet 90 to 100 percent of family need.

https://student.collegeboard.org/css-financial-aid-profile
https://profileonline.collegeboard.org/prf/PXRemote
PartInstitutionServlet/PXRemotePartInstitution
Servlet.srv

In 2017, FAFSA made a major change in their application process. They decided to open the application yearly on October 1ˢᵗ instead of January 1ˢᵗ. It is said to be a positive change not just for schools, but also families. The change allows schools the opportunity to deliver financial aid award letters much earlier so families can make an informed decision on/or by May 1ˢᵗ. Today's typical tuition cost for a college degree ranges from $15,000 – $100,000 per year. Financial Aid and Scholarships are both savings initially, but there is often a balance left to offset the rising cost of tuition. We all have heard the saying "first come first serve basis" well that rings true to financial aid, it is important to complete your application as early as possible in order to maximize the amount of aid you could receive.

All too often, families don't complete the FAFSA because they believe they are not eligible, because they earn too much to qualify for financial aid. On the contrary, they might be surprised to find out they are eligible for some form of reward or federal loans.

Common myths surrounding families completing the FAFSA...

- My parents make too much money, so I won't qualify for aid – False
- I need to file taxes before completing the FAFSA – you can estimate
- My grades aren't good enough to qualify for financial aid
- My ethnicity or age makes me ineligible for financial aid
- The FAFSA is too hard to fill out

Students and parents are responsible for creating a FSA ID, which allows them to "sign" their online FAFSA, make corrections to their application information and keep their information secure **https://studentaid.ed.gov/sa/fafsa/filling-out/fsaid.**

Completing the FAFSA is a prerequisite for unsubsidized Federal Stafford and Federal Plus Loans, Scholarships Grants, and Work-Study...

- **Education Loan Programs:** assist with the educational expenses of the student; including loans from the federal government and private loans from banks and financial institutions

- **Scholarships:** are based on merit (academic), athletic or artistic talent

- **Grants:** are awarded based on financial need or academic achievement and, like scholarships, don't have to be repaid

- **Work Study:** is awarded based on financial need or academic achievement and, like scholarships, don't have to be repaid

When completing the FAFSA be sure to submit all information correctly. If your application contains errors or incomplete responses, the correction process could take weeks. Remember every state has a FAFSA deadline as well as every school **https://fafsa.gov/deadlines.htm.**

When completing the FAFSA you will need the following...

- Your Social Security card and driver's license, and/or alien registration card if you are not a US citizen.

- Your most recent federal income tax returns, W-2's, and other records of money earned. (Note: You may be able to transfer your federal tax return information into your FAFSA by using the IRS data retrieval.

- If you're a dependent (and you are, unless declared otherwise) on your parents' income tax returns, W-2 forms and 1040 forms. If you or your parents have not completed your taxes yet, you can estimate your income and other tax return information, and then correct your application after you have filed your taxes.

- Records and documentation of other untaxed income received such as welfare benefits, Social Security income, veteran's benefits, military or clergy allowances (if applicable).

- Any additional applicable financial information, such as taxable work-study, assistantships, fellowships, grants and scholarship aid reported to the IRS, combat pay or special combat pay and cooperative education program earnings.

- Records of any additional untaxed income examples include: child support received, veterans' non-education benefits, money received or paid on your behalf, etc.

- Current bank and brokerage account statements, including records of stocks, bonds, mutual funds and other investments (if applicable).

- Business or investment farm records (if applicable).

Within two to four weeks after completing the FAFSA the U.S. Department of Education will send you your Student Aid Report (SAR). Review your SAR and, if necessary, make changes or corrections and submit your SAR for reprocessing. Your SAR will contain your Expected Family Contribution (EFC) the number used to determine your federal student aid eligibility. If a student's EFC is less than a college's cost of attendance, then the student qualifies for need-based financial aid. Even if a student qualifies for need-based aid it doesn't mean that the college or university will meet 100% of the student's need.

Note: Your expected family contribution is subject to change – especially depending on whether you have siblings in college, too. Parents often think that having two kids in college at the same time is twice as expensive as having one, but that isn't true. Both school aid and federal grants (but not unsubsidized loans) are based on expected family contribution (EFC), and if there are multiple siblings in college at the same time the EFC is divided by the number of college-aged kids. That's how the Free Application for Federal Student Aid (FAFSA) formula for assessing your need works.

Families are often left trying to answer questions on their own about Financial Aid and Student Loans. One of the first steps is to decide which type of loan is best for you.

Below is an overview as it relates to Federal versus Private Loans...

Federal Perkins Loans: are federally backed loans that are for students demonstrating a financial need (eligible for loan forgiveness through special programs on any student debt remaining after 10 years of qualifying payments for people in government, nonprofit, and other public service jobs after graduation).

Subsidized Stafford Loan: a loan for which the government pays the interest while you are in school, during grace periods, and during any deferment periods – repay six months after you graduate (student responsibility).

Unsubsidized Stafford Loan: are federal loans that do not need proof of financial need, but are limited to how much you can take out each year (responsible for paying all the interest that accrues at any point in time – repay six months after you graduate student responsibility).

Parent Plus Loans: are unsubsidized parent loans – (parent responsibility). If parents cannot obtain a PLUS loan (based on a credit check) students may be eligible to borrow additional unsubsidized funds. Interest rates and repayment plans vary. "Parents should also be aware that if they borrow this year and the next and the next that their loan payments will increase each year as debt accumulates, and they may not be able to handle the increase in monthly loan payments, especially if they have more children enrolling in college in subsequent years."

Private Loans: are available for students who need additional money for college expenses beyond what they have received via financial aid. Private student loans are received through financial establishments, such as banks or community lenders. Interest rates can be higher with private loans and require good credit and/or a cosigner.

Note: private loans are usually not eligible for loan forgiveness programs or federal income-driven repayment plans.

Loan chart at a glance...

	Pros	Cons
Federal PLUS Loan for parents	• The loan covers a student's financial need, minus other aid. • Borrowers qualify simply by having no negative credit history. • No collateral is required or put at risk. • No income restrictions apply. • Repayment can be deferred while the student is enrolled at least halftime. • The interest paid may be tax deductible.	• Loans accrue interest and must be repaid. • The loan is in the parent's name and won't help the students build their credit history.
Cosigning a private student loan	• Private loans help cover college expenses after lower-cost options have been exhausted. • Payments can be deferred while the student is in school. • The student is the primary borrower. • Timely loan repayment may help the student create a good credit history. • Your good credit history often helps ensure a lower interest rate for the student. • The interest paid may be tax deductible.	• Loans accrue interest and must be repaid. • The loan is in the student's name and some parents don't want their students to accrue debt. • Late payments may affect the cosigner's credit report, even if the cosigner isn't the one making payments.

	Pros	Cons
A private student loan for parent borrowers	• Private loans help cover college expenses after lower-cost options have been exhausted. • A parent or other sponsor is the primary borrower. • You could elect to make interest only payments while the student is in school. • The interest paid may be tax deductible.	• Loans accrue interest and must be repaid. • The loan is in the parent's name and won't help students build their credit history.

When researching which loan is right for your family here are a few questions to consider...

- What is the interest rate
- Is the interest rate fixed or variable – Do I have a choice
- Will I need a cosigner
- Are there fees associated
- What are the enrollment requirements
- Will I need to make payments while I'm in school
- Is there a minimum or maximum amount I can borrow
- Does the lender provide/have interest rate reductions or other incentives for borrowers

When applying for loans have the following information ready...

- Your school's information, such as name, address, phone number, and your major
- Your social Security number
- Current mailing address
- Gross income information for both you and the cosigner is needed
- Residence information, including whether you own or rent, and the monthly housing payment
- Requested loan amount

Once you borrow the money remember to do the following...

- **Know Your Loans:** It's important to keep track of the lender, balance, and repayment status for the money you borrow.

- **Know Your Grace Period:** Different loans have different grace periods for how long you can wait after leaving school before you have to make your first payment. It's six months for federal Stafford loans, but nine months for federal Perkins loans. For federal PLUS loans, it depends on when they were issued **https://studentaid.ed.gov/sa/types/loans/plus**. The grace periods for private student loans vary, contact your lender to find out.

- **Stay in Touch with Your Lender:** Keep your information up to date. Open and read all paper or electronic mail you receive about your student loans.

- **Prepay If You Can:** If you can afford to pay on your loans while in school do so. Waiting until graduation only creates more stress. During the summer and breaks work to put money towards paying off your loans.

Note: Remember to be smart in your borrowing and read the fine print to understand the terms and expectations before signing.

At the end of the college admissions and financial aid application process, students will receive an official financial aid award letter from each institution explaining their eligibility for all the aid he/she is eligible for and/or has been awarded; including outside scholarships, state grants, student loans, work-study, etc. The award letter will also include the total cost of attendance to enroll for the upcoming academic year, including tuition, fees, room, board, books, travel and personal expenses. When comparing financial aid award letters from different colleges, calculate the net price (difference between the total cost – grants, scholarships, and other grant aid) of each school. The net price is the amount the family will have to pay from savings, income and loans to cover the cost of college. You may already know how much you will need from your financial aid letter, but understanding what your options are can help put your mind at ease.

In order to come up with the total aid, many colleges mix loans with grants and scholarships. Doing this makes your total "aid award" appear as if you have a low or zero balance, but as you know by now, loans are not gifts. They must be repaid. According to student loan servicer Sallie Mae, nearly two-thirds of families (65%) used grants and scholarships to pay for college in 2013, up from 61% in 2012 and up from only half of families five years ago. What's more, 49% of parents say they're not regularly setting aside money to college savings, and 70% of those parents say the reason they're not saving is because they simply can't afford to. In other words: more and more families are counting on grants and scholarships (including tuition discounts from the school itself) to pay for college.

The net price is more important than the overall cost of attendance. The total cost of attending a school might look high, but when you factor in scholarships and grants, a Costly University might actually be the most affordable school. In the end decide which school to attend based on a combination of (a) how well the school suits your needs and (b) its affordability after all aid is taken into account. Unfortunately, award letters are not as easy to interpret as an acceptance or rejection letter.

Don't hesitate to get free information and help from your school counselor, the financial aid office at the college or career school you plan to attend (to gain a clearer understanding of the type of grants, scholarships and loans they offer), or visit the U.S. Department of Education website at: **www.FederalStudentAid.ed.gov** or 1-800-4-FED-AID (1-800-433-3243).

Remember, making plans about how to pay for college is a family effort. Have a candid conversation to determine how your family will handle financing your education.

Sample Award Letter

Cost of Attendance

Tuition and fees. $10,000

Room and board $8,456

Books and supplies $1,000

Transportation. $1,500

Health insurance/fees $1,000

Miscellaneous/personal $1,500

Total Cost. $23,456

Gift Aid

Grants. $15,000

Resources (outside scholarships) $500

Resources (veterans' education benefits). $1,000

Total Gift Aid. $16,500

OUT OF POCKET COST $6,956

Self Help Aid

Need-based loans. $2,500

Employment (work study). $1,000

Total Self Help Aid $3,500

NET COST $3,456

Non-Need-Based Loans

Federal student loans. $1,000

Federal parent loans. $2,456

Private student loans 0

Total Non-Need-Based Loans $3,456

It's Time To Make A Decision

Drum roll please! Now that the daily mailbox run is over and you have torn open all the letters to receive your acceptances, wait-list, or denial letters, I am sure you hear loud bells ringing as you ponder what's next. As a young adult this is one of the biggest decisions you will make in your life. Take your time and weigh all the pros and cons. Remove all the glitz and glamour from the open houses where they rolled out the red carpet during your visit and remember this will become your home away from home for the next four years.

For some the decision will be tough, because you broke the rules and applied to 10 or more schools. Forgetting that ultimately in the end you can only choose one.

Here are 5 steps to take as you prepare to make your final decision before May 1st...

Step 1: Review your financial aid award letter from all of your accepted schools. Narrow down which two or three schools you see yourself being successful academically, socially and most importantly feels like it can be home for the next four years.

Step 2: Schedule a visit to your top two schools to gain one final look; if possible make it an overnight visit.

Step 3: Decide what's best for your family. Although school choice A might be the school you really want to attend – make sure the school is cost effective and falls within the budget you set with your family. This might sound unfair, but college should not come at the sacrifice of your family. After all school choice B can't be too bad you had it on your list.

Step 4: If money is a factor in making a final decision don't hesitate to contact your school's financial aid office to inquire if they have additional funds they can offer. Now, I am not saying call the school trying to negotiate, they are not a sales lot – let them know your financial concerns and inquire if there are any additional funds available. If you never ask they will never offer.

Step 5: Now that you have made the announcement you should be over joyed! However, there is still one final step: completing your final decision paperwork and mailing it by the May 1st deadline (you don't have to wait until May 1st to mail or complete your paperwork you can do it today). Remember dorm rooms are assigned on a first come basis.

Dear Student

Letters from Suited 4 Success
Shining Stars

Dear Student,

It was my senior year of high school and I didn't know where I was going to attend school in the fall, because I didn't have any offers and my first choice school cost too much. My grandmother signed me up for a college tour with an organization called Suited 4 Success. The tour was for four days. I kept telling her I didn't want to go because it wouldn't make a difference...little did I know this was the extra guidance I needed to expand my range of opportunities. I finally gave in and went on the college trip. I met new people, enjoyed visiting all the schools, staying in hotels etc. This experience allowed me to realize the type of campus that would best suit me.

After coming back from the tour my grandmother signed me up for Suited 4 Success to customized college program, which gave me access to having one-on-one sessions with Ms. Robinson as I completed the college process. Ms. Robinson truly takes the time to get to know her students so she can guide them into making the best choice for themselves. In the program we worked together on the following: choosing seven colleges to apply to, essay writing assistance, review of acceptance letters, creating academic resumes and ensuring I was ready in the end for my chosen institution. In the end I got accepted into all seven of my schools. I applied to; North Carolina A&T University, University of Miami, and Pennsylvania State University just to name a few. Having Ms. Robinson as a resource helped me tremendously. In the end I didn't attend my dream school. With Ms. Robinson's help I got a presidential scholarship to Widener University and was able to walk on as a starting football player my freshman year. None of this would have been possible without the assistance of Ms. Robinson.

Getting into school is only the beginning. Everyone will go through experiences that will test their character. For me it was breaking my femur in a football game and my grades falling due to my injury. Although I recovered from the injury quickly, my GPA was still under a 2.0. After being threatened to get kicked out of the Engineering program, I recovered and came back the next year and earned a 3.0 GPA. However, this was still not enough to keep my scholarship. I knew I still wanted to attend school and earn my degree so I returned home for a semester. I am currently taking classes at a community college earning enough credits to transfer to a four-year institution. Whatever you choose to do always stay in motion.

Respectfully,
Malik Murray
College Student
Community Colllege

Dear Student,

It is okay to not have your life totally planned out. You do not need to know what you are going to do in the next 5, 10, or even 15 years. I am a junior in college and I do not know what I want to do when I graduate. As life goes on you will begin to find out what you like and dislike. Once you have these encounters you will be able to slowly decide which direction you want to take your life.

As you are matriculating through your senior year, I advise you to start the college process early. The earlier you start the less stress that you will have at the end. This includes taking the SAT/ACT, going on college tours, applying for scholarships, and most importantly applying for colleges. However, even if you do not start early it is never too late to begin. In high school, I did very well academically but I did not take the college process seriously. I started applying for colleges and scholarships later than I should have. I always knew I was going to college but I did not care what college I was going to. This attitude that I possessed really backfired on me because I felt like I was playing the catch up game. I spent many nights worrying about where I was going to attend college and how I was going to afford it. I would not have been able to get through this stressful process without Suited 4 Success. Ms. Robinson is one of the most patient and hardworking women I know. She pushed me but also had my back throughout this whole process. From helping me narrow down the schools I was going to apply to, to writing essays, even to writing 15 essays in two days for a scholarship. Ms. Robinson was there every step of the way. I would not have gotten into school without her. Even with my late start, I was blessed to able to get into my top three schools. All my stress could have been avoided if I would have started early. Nevertheless it is never too late to begin your process.

As your acceptance letters begin rolling in it is time to figure out how you are going to pay for college. Whether you are going to community college, a Historically Black College or University (HBCU), a private or public institution either way college is NOT cheap! Your school may give you financial aid or they may not. Regardless of what you receive you should always apply for outside scholarships. When looking for outside scholarships begin by looking within your high school and the clubs/organizations that you are affiliated with. You should also look for scholarships within your local community and nationally. Even if you do not meet all the qualifications for a scholarship it does not hurt to apply. But your main target should be specific scholarships that you are confident you will get. You are most likely not going to receive every scholarship you apply for because the scholarship hunt is very competitive. If you stay consistent and use the resources around you, you will produce a positive outcome.

Now you're transitioning into college, and you are excited but let me be clear; college is not high school! You are not going to be in one building for eight hours a day, nobody is going to wake you up for class, or be on your back about your homework. In college, you are on your own. It is easy to skip class because nobody is making sure you are going unlike when you are in high school. You may find some good friends that hold you accountable nonetheless you are still responsible for your academic success. Managing your time is the key to being successful in college. It will be very easy to procrastinate because you will be afforded more idol time than you have ever had. You have to know yourself and your professors. Knowing your professors is essential because that could determine whether you pass or fail.

Some professors will only grade tests so you know you have to do well on all your tests. Some professors are strict about your attendance and will lower your grade by a letter (i.e. B to C). While other professors do not care about attendance but they will fail you if you do not turn in assignments on time. It honestly just depends on the professor. Going to your professor's office hours will be very beneficial. It can help them get to know you better in case you need a recommendation letter, extra help in class, or it can even help you if need to bump your grade up from a B- to a regular B. Also, studying abroad is something that EVERY college student should take advantage of. Whether you decide to go for a week, two weeks or even an entire semester. The benefits of getting a global experience are unimaginable. There are scholarships and financial aid available to offset the cost of studying abroad; so don't get discouraged.

Lastly, take advantage of all the opportunities presented to you, both now and when you transition into college. I cannot stress enough the importance of starting early. Personally, I started later than I should have. Despite my late start, I always managed to succeed but not without stress and many sleepless nights. It is always important to put your best foot forward in college, so you can set yourself up for success. I have had a very successful college career so far, from interning at Facebook to studying abroad in Seoul, South Korea and Havana, Cuba. One key to success in college is not comparing yourself to the people around you. Your life and what is destined for you is for you and nobody else. Just because your friends may seem to be progressing faster than you think you are does not determine your success. Once it is your time you will know it. Always remember, it is a marathon, not a sprint. Please trust your process and do not rush it. I hope I did not overwhelm you in this letter. Enjoy the end of your high school career. It is okay to make mistakes. Your four years in college will be very monumental so enjoy it to the fullest while remaining focus!

Respectfully,
Nia Michelle Massey
College Student
Spelman College

Dear Student,

The time is now. Reality has begun. For the past 12 years, you've been taught the basics of young adulthood and it is finally here. When I entered the 9th grade, I knew what I wanted to do career wise; however, I had no idea where I wanted to go. A part of me wanted to go so far away and experience life on my own, the other half of me wanted to stay as close to my parents as I possibly could. By the time I reached junior year, I still had no idea, until I attended a college tour with Suited 4 Success that changed my entire life.

I went from falling in love with Spelman, Clark Atlanta and Hampton to falling for what I feel is the BEST Historically Black College there is – North Carolina Central University. If it weren't for the Suited 4 Success college tour, I would be at home not getting the "pre adulthood" experience. When we toured the different universities, I finally realized that Spelman, Clark and Hampton were not the best moves for me. Being on NCCU's campus made me realize that that was where I needed to be. Not too far from home and not too close either was definitely the right decision for me at the age of 17.

When I first got to NCCU, I was ready to go simply because no one really wanted to get to know me or felt like I was "stuck up." I had all of four friends and I was perfectly fine being in my comfort zone. NCCU didn't shape me until the end of my sophomore year.

As a college student, you will meet friends you will have for a lifetime, discover friends that will turn into enemies, and experience what "fake love" really is. However, never lose focus of why you went to college to graduate and make your loved ones proud.

Graduates, never allow anyone to take advantage of you or get in the way of what you are trying to accomplish. Never let anyone get the best of you and take you out of character. Always remember your worth and the person your parents raised you to be.

I went from being an [anti-social] butterfly that lacked confidence and felt as though I didn't have potential, to being a college graduate with honors and all the confidence in the world. Not only did I graduate with my undergraduate degree in four years, I was blessed with so many opportunities right after graduation. From receiving a 10-week internship, to receiving a full time job in my field to getting accepted into one of the top institutions in the United States, Georgetown University. I know it was my faith, hard work and dedication that got me where I am today.

Graduates, never forget where you came from no matter where you go. No matter who raised you or what you've been through, remember you can be so much better than your circumstances. Although I would love to share my whole experience, I know everyone's experiences are different but I encourage you to stay the course. The time has come for you to shine.

Welcome to the real world, where you will discover more of you everyday. I wish each and every one of you reading this letter the best in all your future endeavors.

Respectfully,
A College Graduate & Master's Student
Alexis Kemp
Georgetown University

Dear Student,

Almost eight years ago I embarked upon my journey to college. It was August 2009 in Queens, NY a familiar city but an unfamiliar territory. A million things rushed through my head – excitement, uncertainty, joy, fear, optimism, doubt, and pride. I had prepared all my life for this, but somehow still felt unprepared. The next four years would turn out to be the best and worst experiences of my life. I did not know what was to come, but I was sure it would be a great narrative in the end.

You see, college is just a new chapter in the book of life; we all would like to skip past the plot twists, villain victories and losses to see what happens in the end, but we must sit through the journey to understand the why, when and how. When speaking about my experience I always say that the most valuable lessons I learned in college were not those taught to me in the classroom or read in a textbook, but through the experiences I encountered when dealing with people from different cultures and different walks of life. College is an incubator of sorts, a place where dreams, passions and desires are explored, skilled and perfected. It is an environment where you get to discover the possibilities of the world, not only through your eyes, but the eyes of your fellow students, faculty and staff. Take your time, explore, try new things, hang out with new people, work hard, play hard, and WOW (Work On Winning)!

As an entrepreneur I built my resilience, drive and fearless spirit on the backs of the tough lessons I learned in college. When they told me there wasn't enough money, I made a way; when they told me the class or group wasn't available, I created it; when things weren't right I learned to stand up and demand change; when people quit I had the confidence to step in and lead, even if I wasn't sure how I was going to get it done.

College gave me time, space and opportunity, but it was only made possible through my preparation and drive to succeed. In high school I made a conscious effort to position myself to not only attend college, but to succeed and finish. I researched schools, signed up for visits, met with counselors, studied, kept my grades up, volunteered, participated in after-school activities, completed practice tests, etc. Although I did not attend my dream school (because I couldn't afford it), but as luck would have it I still ended up at a school I couldn't afford but my grades paid the way literally! And I took advantage of the opportunity and got the most I could out of my experience.

I stand here today after pulling all-nighters, studying at work, after work, in class and out; passing exams, and failing some; doing group projects that turned into solo projects and finishing the internship from hell, as a full-time entrepreneur and first generation college student, all because I saw all the possibilities life had to offer in college. Yes I earned a bachelors degree with honors, was inducted into two honors societies and had several appearances on the dean's list; but I also built character, integrity, selflessness and compassion for people that is unmatched. College made me an all around better person, which in the end is PRICELESS.

CROWND,
A College Graduate
J. Dyson
CEO P2P Branded

••••••••••••••••••

College

Bound

Resources

••••••••••••••••••

Scholarship Resources

September Scholarships

Heather Burns Scholarship
(College Students)
September 22
http://www.hbmsf.org/thehbmsfscholarship.html

National College Match Scholarship
(High School Seniors)
September 27
http://www.questbridge.org/for-students/ncm-national-college-match

Evans Scholarship Application
(High School Juniors or above)
September 30
http://www.wgaesf.org/site/c.dwJTKiO0J-gI8G/b.6021361/k.8BED/WGAESF_Home.htm

Xerox Technical Minority Scholarship
(College Students)
September 30
http://www.xerox.com/jobs/minority-scholarships/enus.html

Hit the Books Scholarship
(College Students)
September 30
http://www.coffeeforless.com/scholarship

Shout it Out Scholarship
(13 years or older)
September 30
https://www.unigo.com/scholarships/our-scholarships/shout-it-out-scholarship#/fromscholarshipexperts

October Scholarships

Anders Tjellstrom Scholarship
(High School Seniors and College Students)
October 1
http://www.cochlear.com/wps/wcm/connect/us/recipients/baha-4/
baha-4-support-and-community/scholarships/scholarship-details/
scholarships

Asian Women in Business Scholarship
(College Students)
October 1
http://www.awib.org/index.cfm?fuseaction=page.viewPage&page-
ID=811&nodeID=1

Financial Success for Single Mothers Scholarship
(College Students)
October 1
http://www.furzymarketing.com/scholarships/

Graeme Clark Scholarship
(College Students)
October 1
http://www.cochlear.com/wps/wcm/connect/us/recipients/
nucleus-5/nucleus-5-support-and-community/scholarships/
scholarship-details/scholarships

Jack Kent Cooke Young Artist Award
(Ages 8-18)
October 1
http://www.fromthetop.org/programs/scholarships/jack-
kent-cooke-young-artist-award/

Legal Leaders of Tomorrow Scholarship
(College Students)
October 1
http://www.paralegal411.org/scholarship/

Raymond Davis Scholarship
(College Students)
October 1
http://www.imaging.org/ist/membership/davis.cfm?AwardCode=RS

Save the Frogs! Art Contest
(Anyone)
October 1
http://www.savethefrogs.com/art/

Students with Heart Scholarship
(College Students)
October 1
http://www.studentswithheart.org/scholarships.html

Wendy's High School Heisman Award
(High School Seniors)
October 2
https://www.wendyshighschoolheisman.com/

WRLA Scholarship
(College Students)
October 2
http://www.wrla.org/education-a-training/bursaries-and-scholarships

Wendy's Heisman Scholarship
(High School Seniors: Student Athletes)
October 2
https://www.whshapplication.com/default.aspx?comp_
id=0E905E28-B2BB-4D65-872D-C407A2887E2A

Rhodes Scholarship
(College Students)
October 2
http://www.rhodesscholar.org/applying-for-the-scholarship/

Snap Scholars Digital Marketing Scholarship
(College Students)
October 5
http://www.snapagency.com/blog/scholarship-contest/

Benjamin A. Gilman International Scholarship
(Undergraduates)
October 6
http://www.iie.org/en/Programs/Gilman-Scholarship-Program

AES Engineering Scholarship
(College Students and High School Seniors)
October 7
http://www.aesengineers.com/scholarships.htm

Jan Egerton and Don Smitley Mesothelioma Scholarship
(College Students)
October 9
http://www.mesotheliomahelp.org/scholarship-contest/

BEA Scholarship
(College Students)
October 13
http://www.beaweb.org/wp/?page_id=478

Future Engineers Scholarship
(College Students)
October 14
http://www.kellyservices.us/EngineeringScholarships/?terms=
scholarships#.Va5soPlVikp

2015 National Rice Month Scholarship Program
(High School Seniors)
October 15
http://usarice.com/all-about-rice/national-rice-month

CIA Internship Program
(High School Seniors and College Students)
October 15
https://www.cia.gov/careers/student-opportunities

Branson Shows Inspired Scholarship
(Ages 16-19)
October 15
http://www.bransonshowtickets.com/company/scholarship.aspx

CIA Undergraduate Scholarship Program
(College Students and High School Seniors)
October 15
https://www.cia.gov/careers/student-opportunities/undergraduate-scholarship-program.html

CJ Pony Parts Scholarship Video Contest
(All Students)
October 15
http://www.cjponyparts.com/cj-pony-parts-scholarship-video-contest

Doodle 4 Google
(All Students)
October 15
http://www.google.com/doodle4google/

Financial Growth for LGBTQ Scholarship
(College Students)
October 15
http://www.johnson-moo.com/lgbtq-scholarship/

Future Engineers Scholarship Program
(College Students)
October 15
http://www.kellyservices.us/EngineeringScholarships/?terms=
scholarship

General Scholarship for Higher Learning
(Ages 16 and up)
October 15
http://www.hotelscheap.org/scholarship/apply

Get Educated Online College Scholarship
(High School Students)
October 15
http://www.geteducated.com/free-college-scholarships/
20-distance-learning-scholarships

Helicopter 2050 Challenge
(Ages 9-16)
October 15
http://www.helicopter2050.com/?opt=contest-about

Hispanic Heritage Youth Awards
(Anyone)
October 15
http://hhfawards.hispanicheritage.org/2013/forms/mailing.php

Interior-Deluxe Scholarship Program
(College Students)
October 15
http://www.interior-deluxe.com/content/57-scholarship-program

JEN Scholarships
(High School and College Students)
October 15
http://www.jazzednet.org/node/1300

Ruth Abernathy Presidential Scholarship
(College Students)
October 15
http://www.shapeamerica.org/scholarships/
abernathyscholarship.cfm

SmileMarketing Dental Scholarship
(College Students)
October 15
http://www.smilemarketing.com/dental-scholarship/

YoungArts Program
(Ages 15- 18)
October 16
http://www.youngarts.org/apply

College Jumpstart Scholarship
(10th- 12th graders)
October 17
http://www.jumpstart-scholarship.net/

Dr. Pepper Tuition Giveaway
(Ages 18-24)
October 19
http://www.drpeppertuition.com/

Atlas Shrugged Essay Contest
(College Students and High School Seniors)
October 23
https://www.aynrand.org/students/essay-contests#atlasshrugged-1

Williams- Mystic/ Joseph Conrad Ocean Essay Contest
(College Students and High School Seniors)
October 23
http://mystic.williams.edu/conradcontest/

Horatio Alger Scholarship
(High School Seniors)
October 25
https://www.horatioalger.org/scholarships/apply.cfm

AACN Partnership & Student Scholarship Program
(College Students)
October 31
https://www.certifiedbackground.com/solutions/scholarships.php

Coca-Cola Scholarship
(High School Seniors)
October 31
http://www.coca-colascholarsfoundation.org/applicants/
#.Va5l_vlVikp

Junior Achievement Essay Scholarship
(High School Students)
October 31
http://www.myja.org/students/essay/application/

Disney Dreamers Academy
(All High School Students)
October 31
https://www.disneydreamersacademy.com/

American Buillon Scholarship Program
(College Students)
October 31
https://www.americanbullion.com/scholarship/

Best Value Schools STEM Scholarship for Women
(College Students)
October 31
http://www.bestvalueschools.com/stem-scholarship-for-women/

Buildium's Women in Technology Scholarship
(College Students)
October 31
http://www.buildium.com/women-in-technology-scholarship/

CARiD Scholarship
(Ages 16-20)
October 31
http://www.carid.com/scholarships.html

GTFO Scholarship
(Anyone)
October 31
https://www.dosomething.org/campaigns/GTFO

MyProjectorLamps Scholarship
(College Students and High School Seniors)
October 31
http://www.myprojectorlamps.com/scholarships.html

National Poetry Competition
(Ages 17 and up)
October 31
http://poetrysociety.org.uk/competitions/
national-poetry-competition/

Zombie Apocalypse Scholarship
(Ages 13 and up)
October 31
https://www.unigo.com/scholarships/our-scholarships/zom-
bie-apocalypse-scholarship

November Scholarships

National AIDS Memorial Scholarship
(High School Seniors & College Students)
November 1
http://www.aidsmemorial.org/news-and-resources/young-leaders-scholarship-program-renamed-in-honor-of-aids-educator-activist-and-real-world-star-pedro-zamora

Ron Brown Scholarship
(High School Seniors)
November 2 or January 9
https://www.unigo.com/scholarships/all/ron-brown-scholarship/1025

Bluetooth Breakthrough Award
(All Students)
November 2
https://www.bluetooth.org/en-us/news-events/bluetooth-breakthrough-awards

Jack Kent Cooke
(High School Seniors)
November 4
http://www.jkcf.org/scholarship-programs/college-scholarship/

Prudential Spirit Awards
(Grades 5-12)
November 4
http://spirit.prudential.com/view/page/soc

Stokes Educational Scholarships
(Seniors: Computers Science/ Engineering Major)
November 15
https://www.nsa.gov/careers/opportunities_4_u/students/stokes.shtml

First Freedom Scholarship
(High School Students)
November 17
http://www.thevalentine.org/exhibitions/permanent/valentine-first-freedom-center/for-the-classroom/first-freedom-student-competition/#

Vanguard Minority Scholarship
(College Juniors and Seniors)
November 30
http://blackstudents.blacknews.com/opportunities/vanguard_minority_scholarship.html#.VFe5YyZ0zIU

December Scholarships

Google Scholarship
(Female High School Seniors and College Freshman)
December 2
https://www.google.com/edu/scholarships/the-generation-goo-gle-scholarship/

NREIP OR SEAP
10-Week Paid Internship
December 19
http://nreip.asee.org/
https://seap.asee.org/

Foot Locker Scholar Athletes Program
(All High School Students)
December 19
http://www.footlocker.com/promotion/pro-moId:5002664/?SID=5403&inceptor=1&cm_mmc=SEM-_-Non-Branded-_-Dynamic+Search-_-Google&g-clid=Cj0KEQjw27etBRDA3-ux4p3c58EBEiQAkJzTAKWcYQM-6WwNnoxNwohgHfSNXWlj60C6c3nWhBkVFi4caApra8P8HAQ

Thermo Scientific Pierce Scholarship
(College Students)
December 31
https://www.lifetechnologies.com/us/en/home/life-science/antibod-ies/thermo-scientific-pierce-scholarship-program.html

Moolah Spot Scholarship
(16 years or older)
December 31
http://www.moolahspot.com/scholarship/index.cfm

January Scholarships

Fire Essay Contest
(High School Junior & Seniors)
January 1
https://www.thefire.org/student-network/essay-contest/
Prince George's County Alumnae Chapter Delta Sigma Theta
Sorority, INC.

(High School Students)
January 3
http://www1.pgcps.org/uploadedFiles/Schools_and_Centers/High_
Schools/Potomac/PGCAC2014HSApplic-2013-14.pdf

Courage Essay Contest
(High School Students)
January 6
http://www.jfklibrary.org/Education/Profile-in-Courage-Es-
say-Contest/Eligibility-and-Requirements.aspx

Ron Brown Scholarship
(High School Seniors)
January 9
https://www.ronbrown.org/Media/Default/MediaGalleries/
ApplicationPDFs/2015_Ron_Brown_Scholarship_Application.pdf

2016 GE-Reagan Foundation
(High School Seniors)
January 9
http://www.reaganfoundation.org/GE-RFScholarships.aspx

Burger King Scholarship
(High School Students)
January 10
http://www.nerdwallet.com/nerdscholar/scholarships/view/burg-
er-king-scholars-program-general-track/104

Students of Integrity Essay Contest
(High School Juniors and Seniors)
January 14
http://nehs.4j.lane.edu/wp-content/uploads/2013/10/
Scholarship-List-12-16-14.pdf

Gates Millennium Scholarship
(High School Seniors)
January 14
http://www.gmsp.org/

Tom Joyner Foundation Scholarship
DOT Summer Transportation Internship
(College Students)
January 16
http://www.fhwa.dot.gov/education/stipdg.cfm

Mickey Leland Fellowship
(College Students)
January 18
http://orise.orau.gov/mlef/applicants/eligibility.html

Ronald McDonald Scholarship
(High School Seniors)
January 21
http://www.rmhc.org/rmhc-us-scholarships

Emma L. Bowen Internship
(High School Seniors and College Freshman)
January 31
http://www.emmabowenfoundation.com/index.php/about-our-
program/student-selection-process.html

February Scholarships

APS Minority Scholarship
(High School Seniors and College Students)
February 7
http://www.aps.org/programs/minorities/honors/scholarship/

Jimmy Rane Foundation Scholarship
(High School Seniors and College Students)
February 8
http://www.jimmyranefoundation.org/scholarships/
2-uncategorised/29-jimmy-rane-foundation-scholarship-
eligibility-criteria

The Davidson Fellows Scholarship
(High School Students)
February 11
http://www.davidsongifted.org/fellows/

National Co-Op Scholarship Program
(High School Students)
February 15
http://scholarshipmentor.com/national-co-op-scholarship-program

Jack and Jill of America
(High School Seniors and College Students)
February 15
http://jackandjillinc.org/

Jackie Robinson Foundation
(High School Seniors)
February 15
http://www.jackierobinson.org/

PGC Scholarship Fund
(High School Seniors)
February 15
http://www.pgcjackandjill.org/Chapter_Scholarships.html

Vegetarian Resource Scholarship
(High School Students)
February 20
https://www.vrg.org/student/scholarship_form.pdf

Buick Achievers Scholarship Programs
(All Students)
February 27
http://www.buickachievers.com/

Green Small Business Scholarship
(High School Seniors, College Freshman and Sophomores)
February 28
https://www.yourgreenpal.com/scholarship

March Scholarships

American Chemical Society
(High School Seniors and College Students)
March 1
http://www.acs.org/content/acs/en.html

Diversity in Vision Research Internship
(College Students)
March 1
https://nei.nih.gov/training/diversity_in_research

The Sunflower Initiative
(Female High School Seniors)
March 2
http://www.thesunflowerinitiative.com/

"Frame My Future" Scholarship
(College Students)
March 6
http://www.diplomaframe.com/contests/frame-my-future-scholarship-contest-2015.aspx

Kohl's Cares Scholarship
(Ages 6- 18)
March 15
https://kohls.scholarshipamerica.org/reminder/index.php

Anthem Essay Contest
(8th graders to High School Sophomores)
March 20
http://essaycontest.aynrandnovels.org/Anthem.aspx

College of Pharmacy Summer Program
(High School Juniors and Seniors)
March 20
http://healthsciences.howard.edu/education/colleges/pharmacy/
center-excellence/components/summer-enrichment/high-
school-academy

Quest-Bridge College Prep Scholarship
(Juniors)
March 25
http://www.questbridge.org/

AOWCGWA Scholarship
(Seniors)
March 27
http://www.aowcgwa.org/index.cfm?action=page&page=21

April/May Scholarships

Fountainhead Essay Contest
(Juniors and Seniors)
April 26
http://essaycontest.aynrandnovels.org/TheFountainhead.aspx

Nordstrom Scholar Program
(High School Juniors)
May 1
http://shop.nordstrom.com/c/nordstrom-cares-scholarship

Joseph A. Beaver Scholarship
(Seniors - Washington D.C.)
May 1
www.upo.org/service/beavers-scholarship

Deadlines Vary

Joe Foss Scholarships
(All Students)
Depends on the Scholarship
Deadlines Vary
http://www.joefossinstitute.org/jfi-scholarship-program/

Actuary Scholarships
(All Students)
Deadlines Vary
http://beanactuary.org/study/?fa=scholarship

Walmart Scholarship
(High School Seniors and College Students)
Deadlines Vary
http://foundation.walmart.com/our-focus/associate-scholarships

The Scholarship Experts
(All Students)
Deadlines Vary
https://www.unigo.com/scholarships

Congressional Black Caucus Foundation Scholarships
(Grade Level Varies)
Deadlines Vary
http://www.cbcfinc.org/cbcf-scholarships.html

Woman in Mathematics Essay Contest
(6th grade to College Undergraduates)
Deadlines Vary
https://sites.google.com/site/awmmath/programs/essay-contest

Programs

CBCF Programs
(High School Students and College Students)
Deadlines Vary
http://www.cbcfinc.org/images/stories/LIPSBrochureFinal.pdf

UNCF
(All Students)
Deadlines Vary
https://scholarships.uncf.org/

Federal Diversity Internship
(All Students)
Deadlines Vary
http://www.twc.edu/internships/additional-programs/federal-diversity-internship-initiative

Competitive Government Program
(All Students)
Deadlines Vary
http://www.twc.edu/node/11071

Scholarship Website Resources:

http://www.fastweb.com/
http://scholarshipamerica.org/
http://www.cksf.org/
https://www.chegg.com/schools?zinch=1
http://www.dellscholars.org/
https://www.cappex.com/
https://www.scholarshipexperts.com/
http://www.meritaid.com/
http://www.thurgoodmarshallfund.net/
http://www.uncf.org/
Scholly – app – smart phones

Scholarship Application Checklist

- Completed Application
- Picture
- Official Transcript
- Letters of Recommendation
- Academic Resume
- Essay

Scholarship Chart

Scholarship Name	Materials Needed	Due Date

College Resources

College Admissions

Campus Tours Online	http://www.campustours.com/
Smart College Visit	http://www.smartcollegevisit.com/
Your Campus 360	http://www.youvisit.com/
CollegeXpress	http://www.collegexpress.com/
College Week Live	http://www.collegeweeklive.com/
College Board	https://www.collegeboard.org/
Common Application	https://www.commonapp.org/ Login
HBCU Common Application	http://www.eduinconline.com/
Universal College Application	https://www.universalcollegeapp.com/
Colleges that Change Lives	http://www.ctcl.org/
Petersons Guide	http://www.petersons.com/
College Prowler	https://www.collegeprowler.com/
College Admissions	http://collegeadmissions.testmasters.com/
College Confidential	http://www.collegeconfidential.com/
College Navigator	http://nces.ed.gov/collegenavigator/
US News and World Report	http://colleges.usnews.rankingsandreviews.com/best-colleges
Virtual College Tours	http://ecampustours.com/
College Profiles of over 70000 colleges and universities	http://www.globalroutes.org/
College Options	https://www.mycollegeoptions.org/

Maryland Higher Education Commission	http://www.mhec.state.md.us/
College Completion	http://collegecompletion.chronicle.com/
College Realty Check	https://collegerealitycheck.com/
College Results Online	http://www.collegeresults.org/
The College Solution	http://www.thecollegesolution.com/welcome/
Career One Stop	http://www.careeronestop.org/
College Majors 101	http://www.collegemajors101.com/
My Future	http://www.myfuture.com/
My Next Move	https://www.mynextmove.org/
Occupational Outlook Handbook	http://www.bls.gov/ooh/
O*NET	https://www.onetonline.org/
Pharmacy Is Right for Me	http://pharmacyforme.org/
Road trip Nation	http://roadtripnation.com/
USA Jobs	https://www.usajobs.gov/
What Can I Do with This Major?	http://www.myplan.com/majors/what-to-do-with-a-major.php/

Financial Planning

FAFSA	https://fafsa.ed.gov/
Fastweb	http://www.fastweb.com/
Finaid	http://www.finaid.org/
CSS/Financial Aid	http://student.collegeboard.org/css-financial-aid-profile
Federal Student Aid	https://studentaid.ed.gov/
FedMoney	http://fedmoney.org/
Scholarship Experts	https://www.scholarshipexperts.com/
Saving for College	http://www.savingforcollege.com/
Financial Aid News	http://www.financialaidnews.com/
Merit Aid Scholarship Search	http://www.meritaid.com/
National Association of Student Financial Aid Administrators	http://www.nasfaa.org/
Federal Direct Loans	http://www.direct.ed.gov/
Federal Student Aid	https://studentaid.ed.gov/
Financial Aid Calculator	http://www.finaid.org/calculators/
DCTAG - OSSE	http://osse.dc.gov/service/dc-tuition-assistance-grant-dc-tag/
Thurgood Marshall Scholarship Fund	http://www.thurgoodmarshall-fund.net/
United Negro College Fund	http://www.uncf.org/
US Department of Education	http://www.ed.gov/
Cappex	https://www.cappex.com/
Edvisors	https://www.edvisors.com/
EFC Calculator	https://bigfuture.collegeboard.org/pay-for-college/paying-your-share/expected-family-contribution-calculator
Tuition Tracker	http://www.tuitiontracker.org/

Testing

ACT	http://www.actstudent.org/
SAT	https://www.collegeboard.org/
AP Exams	https://apstudent.collegeboard.org/home
TOEFL Exams	http://www.ets.org/toefl?WT.ac=toefl-home_why_121127
ASVAB	http://official-asvab.com/
Number2	https://www.number2.com/

Learning Disabilities

"Americans" with Disabilities Act	http://www.ada.gov/
Attention Deficit Disorder Association	http://www.chadd.org/
Council for Exceptional Children	http://www.chadd.org/
Learning Disabilities Association of America	http://ldaamerica.org/
LD Resources	http://www.ldresources.com/
National Center for Learning Disabilities	http://www.ncld.org/
Smart Kids with Learning Disabilities	http://www.smartkidswithld.org/
Disability Friendly Colleges	http://www.disabilityfriendlycolleges.com/

Student Athletes

NCAA	http://www.ncaa.org/
NAIA	http://naia.org/
NCAA Clearinghouse	http://web1.ncaa.org/ECWR2/ NCAA_EMS/NCAA_EMS.html
National Scouting Report	http://nsr-inc.com/
National Association of Collegiate Directors of Athletics	http://www.nacda.com/
The College Planning Guide for Athletes	https://www.nhheaf.org/pdfs/athlet-icbooklet.pdf

Recommendation Letter Template

Date

Dear _____:

I would like to take this opportunity to ask you to write letters of recommendation for my College and Scholarship Applications. Please type all recommendations on school letterhead with my full name at the top.

Enclosed is a copy of my academic resume listing my achievements and activities during my high school career.

Please complete and return the letters of recommendation by **Date.** With your permission, I would like to keep a copy on file for the next year as I complete my post-secondary plans.

If you have any questions, please do not hesitate to contact me at **Phone Number** or **Email**.

Words cannot express how much I appreciate the time and effort you will put into writing my recommendation letters.

Sincerely,

Full Name
Class of _____

Academic Resume Template

Name
Full Address
Contact Number
Email

Education
High School Name
Cumulative GPA:
SAT Scores:
ACT Scores
Academic Courses:
Electives Completed:

Volunteer Experience

Name of Organization	Number of Hours	Date

Extracurricular Activities

Name of Organization	Number of Hours	Date

Honors Received

Name of Honors		Date

Skills

My Key-Chain

Name: _____

Website: _____

Username: _____

Password:_____

Name: _____

Website: _____

Username: _____

Password: _____

Name: _____

Website: _____

Username: _____

Password: _____

Name: _____

Website: _____

Username: _____

Password: _____

Name: _____

Website: _____

Username: _____

Password:_____

Name: _____

Website: _____

Username: _____

Password: _____

Name: _____

Website: _____

Username: _____

Password:_____

Name: _____

Website: _____

Username: _____

Password: _____

Name: _____

Website: _____

Username: _____

Password: _____

Name: _____

Website: _____

Username: _____

Password: _____

College Fair Questions

Introduction: A good way to start is by introducing yourself and your field of interest. Then follow up with, "What sets your college apart from others?"

- What does your school consider for admissions? (Examples: activities, grades, SAT/ACT scores)
- What is the annual cost of your school? (Examples: tuition, room and board, etc.)
  - o What kind of financial aid does your school offer and is there a deadline?
  - o Scholarships (do they require a separate application or are students automatically qualified once they complete an application)?
  - o Does your school offer grants to incoming students?
- Does your school offer student housing, if so, is it guaranteed all four years?
- What is the student-to-teacher ratio at your school?
- Does your school offer support services, peer counseling, job placement, internships, study abroad programs, tutoring, and career development?

Closing: May I please have a business card with your direct number to keep in contact with you in case I have further questions?

College Admissions Interview

Interview Questions

Practicing these questions will give you the confidence to master your interview. Remember it is important to relax and have a conversation with your interviewer(s).

How have you been a leader or displayed leadership?
Don't just list titles and positions, focus on a specific leadership position or activity and give details that express your commitment. You don't have to hold a title to show leadership.

What is your greatest strength and weakness?
Use a specific example to highlight your strength and leadership. Share how you led, the results and why you enjoyed it? If you have a weakness express it with honesty, but most importantly show how you're working to overcome that weakness. Make sure the interviewer knows your weakness will not keep you from being a successful college student.

Why did you choose this college?
Explain why their college is important to you (For example: how you plan to utilize their research facilities to enhance your education) walk the interviewer through your thinking process when selecting their school.

Why do you want to enter this career?
What inspires you to pursue this area of study? You can answer simply by talking about an experience, speaker, book or TV show that inspired you.

If you could do one thing in high school differently, what would it be?
Don't dwell on things you regret. Instead express positive examples: maybe you would have liked to take classes in acting, music or participate in the school newspaper.

Interview Questions "ASK"

The interviewer will ask, do you have any questions or anything to add? Absolutely, here are some sample questions. Choose two or three to ask.

Sample questions:

- What would a graduate of your college say was the most valuable lesson about their four years here at your school?

- What can you tell me that I cannot read or find on your website?

- What advice would you give me as an incoming freshman?

- I notice that a program you're interested in has these benefits, criteria, rewards, etc. for students. Can you tell me more about it/them?

- What does the college do to assist students with career planning, internships, and future job placement?

Interview Do's & Don'ts

Complete your interview with a firm handshake and a follow up thank you email.

Interview:

DO's...

- Research the school
- Dress appropriately (business casual)
- Be on time (arrive 15 minutes early)
- Hand firm shake
- Make eye contact
- Speak clearly
- Answer questions with clarity

DON'TS...

- Be Late
- Under dress
- Talk Too Little
- Make a Prepared Speech
- Chew Gum
- Bring Your Parents in the room (unless they specify)
- Show Disinterest (by making comments like "you're my back-up school" or "I'm here because my parents told me to apply")
- Fail to Research the College (don't ask questions that could easily be answered by the college's website)
- Lie

Frequently Asked Questions

Financial Aid

When should I fill out the FAFSA?

You must complete the FAFSA yearly in the month of October **http://fafsa.gov/**

Do parents have to wait to complete the FAFSA after they have filed their income taxes?

No, they can estimate.

Is there a different deadline by state for completing the FAFSA?

Yes, every state has a deadline – it is important to check your state and the state your schools are located to determine their deadline date.

What is a SAR report?

A Student Aid Report summarizes the data from your completed FAFSA and indicates your estimated expected family contribution.

When should I create my (student and parent) FSA ID?

You can create you FSA ID at anytime. Be sure to keep your login information in a safe place. Just go the following website: **https://studentaid.ed.gov/sa/fafsa/filling-out/fsaid**.

If a parent has a child in college or have completed the FAFSA for themselves will they need to create a FSA ID?

No, they can use their current FSA ID.

How many scholarships should a student apply for?

Students should apply to as many scholarships as possible.

College Admissions

When is the best time to begin the college planning process?
Your sophomore or junior year of high school is the best time to begin preparing your college list, action plan, and schedule.

Should students attend college fairs?
Students should start attending college fairs as early as their freshman year in high school.

Should students involve parents in their college selection process?
Yes, high school is not a time to go on autopilot. In fact this is a crucial time for parents to support their children.

What should students do when asking a teacher and counselor for a recommendation letter?
Students should provide their teacher and counselor with a formal written request, a copy of their resume, a list of schools, and most importantly at least a two-week turn around time.

How many schools should a student apply?
Students should create a balanced list of 5-7 schools.

When is a college application considered completed by an admissions office?
When you complete an online or paper application, submit an application fee, official transcript, official SAT/ACT scores through **www.collegeboard.com** and **www.act.org,** recommendation letters, an essay and supporting supplemental documents.

When should a student mail their college applications?
Students should mail their applications by Thanksgiving break, but no later than Christmas break.

College Admissions Continued…

Do colleges review senior year grades?
All colleges will request a final transcript from students.

Do colleges accept fee waivers?
Some schools welcome fee waivers. If you are a free or reduced lunch student you qualify to receive fee waivers for testing and applications.

What is the difference between early decision and early action?
Early Decision: is a binding agreement between the student and the accepting college or university. If a student is accepted, he/she must attend that college or university. An agreement binding the student to the school upon acceptance is required prior to submitting the Early Decision application and is signed by the student, parent, and guidance counselor.

Early Action: is a non-binding early decision process, typically requiring students to submit an application by November 1st of their senior year of high school. The Early Action Decision is provided to the student by mid-December.

What is EDU, Inc.?
EDU, Inc. is a Common Black College Application that allows students to apply to thirty-six Historically Black Colleges for a one-time application fee of $35.00 visit: **http://www.eduinconline.com**.

What is the Common Application?
The Common Application is a not-for-profit organization that serves students and member institutions by providing an online admission application students may submit to any of the member schools: **https://www.commonapp.org/Login**.

Testing

When should students take the SAT/ACT for the first time?
Students should take the SAT and ACT their junior year. This will give students the opportunity to improve their weaknesses by the first scheduled test of their senior year. Register for the SAT test at: **http://www.collegeboard.com** and for the ACT test at: **http://actstudent.org.**

What is the difference between the SAT and ACT?
Many educators believe that the SAT evaluates critical thinking and problem solving while the ACT is based on specific content and curriculum. Most colleges accept either test, while some colleges require SAT subject tests. Nearly 850+ colleges are test-optional and do not require either the SAT or ACT.

What is the average SAT score per section?
The average score is 500+ for Math and Reading.

What are the average ACT scores schools are looking for?
The average score is 21+ and above.

If a student does not score well on the SAT, will he or she get into a good college, right?
Colleges use a "holistic" approach to evaluate applications for admission. Along with the test scores, they also consider the student's grade point average, whether or not the student is enrolling in challenging courses, extra-curricular activities, letters of recommendation and leadership roles the student has undertaken in high school. Some colleges have become "test optional", which allows students to be admitted based on a high grade point average or additional letters of recommendation.

Student
Dorm CHECKLIST

CHECKLIST.

✓ Everything you're going to need!

BEDDING & ACCESSORIES

- ○ COMFORTER (down or alternative)
- ○ BED PILLOWS/PROTECTOR
- ○ MATTRESS PAD
- ○ MATTRESS TOPPER
- ○ 2-3 LARGE SHEET SETS
- ○ THROW/BLANKET

DESK ORGANIZATION

- ○ DESK/CLIP LAMP
- ○ LIGHT BULBS
- ○ DESK ORGANIZERS
- ○ MESSAGE/BULLETIN BOARD
- ○ CALENDAR

BATH

- ○ TOWELS/WASHCLOTHS
- ○ SHOWER TOTE/CADDY
- ○ FLIP-FLOPS/SHOWER SHOES
- ○ TOOTHBRUSH/SOAP CASE
- ○ MESH SPONGE
- ○ RUG

PERSONAL CARE & GROOMING

- ○ TOOTHBRUSH
- ○ HAIR BRUSH
- ○ HAIR CARE CADDY
- ○ HAIR DRYER
- ○ HAIR STRAIGHTENER/STYLER
- ○ SHAVER
- ○ FACE MIRROR

STORAGE & ORGANIZATION

- ◯ STORAGE CART
- ◯ DRAWER ORGANIZER
- ◯ ADHESIVE HOOKS
- ◯ SHELVING
- ◯ DUFFEL BAG/BACKPACK
- ◯ STORAGE TRUNK

OVER THE DOOR

- ◯ CAP/PURSE ORGANIZER
- ◯ DOOR MIRROR
- ◯ HOOKS/HOOK RAGS
- ◯ SHOE STORAGE

UNDER THE BED

- ◯ ZIPLOC SPACE BAGS
- ◯ STACKING DRAWERS

READY FOR ANYTHING?

- ◯ BATTERIES
- ◯ FIRST AID KIT
- ◯ FLASHLIGHT
- ◯ TOOL KIT

ELECTRONICS & AUDIO

- ◯ SURGE PROTECTOR
- ◯ EXTENSION CORD
- ◯ USB WALL ADAPTERS
- ◯ PHONE CHARGER
- ◯ ALARM CLOCK
- ◯ ETHERNET CABLE
- ◯ TV & CABLES

LAUNDRY & CLEANING

- ◯ LANDRY BASKET
- ◯ LANDRY DETERGENT
- ◯ TOWEL RACK
- ◯ IRON/STEAMER
- ◯ IRONING BOARD
- ◯ TRASHCAN
- ◯ CLEANING CLOTH/WIPES
- ◯ VACCUM
- ◯ BROOM/DUSTPAN

YOU'RE ALMOST ON YOUR WAY!

KITCHEN TOOLS & DINING

- ◯ PLATES & BOWLS
- ◯ CUPS & MUGS
- ◯ EATING UTENSILS
- ◯ WATER BOTTLE
- ◯ FOOD STORAGE
- ◯ BAG/CHIP CLIPS
- ◯ CAN OPENER

ROOM DECOR

- ◯ DECORATIVE PILLOWS
- ◯ FLOOR LAMP
- ◯ WALL ART
- ◯ AREA RUG
- ◯ FAN
- ◯ ROOM FRAGRANCES
- ◯ PICTURE BOARD

WAIT I ALMOST FORGOT!

- ◯ _____
- ◯ _____
- ◯ _____
- ◯ _____

- ◯ _____
- ◯ _____
- ◯ _____
- ◯ _____

AND SO MUCH MORE‼

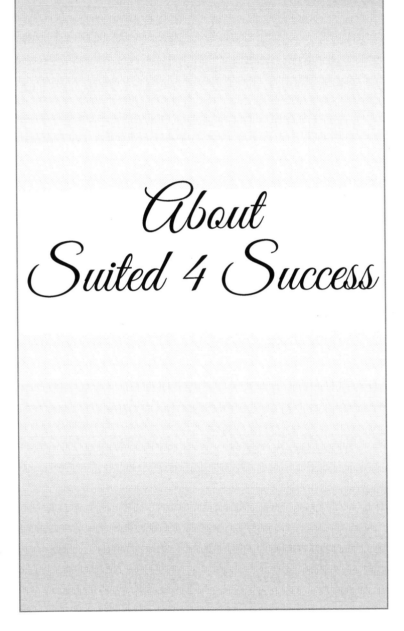

About
Suited 4 Success

About Us

Getting into college is more competitive than ever and at the same time, the cost of college is rising dramatically. Suited for Success has been providing comprehensive college admissions counseling for families since 2002. Our mission is to ensure our students understand that education is the pathway to every young person's life – where they explore their aspirations and learn what empowers them through their voice, experiences, networking and knowledge.

Suited 4 Success is recognized for its expertise, excellent track record and collaborative counseling approach in motivating and empowering students to reach their academic and personal goals while eliminating the stress commonly associated with the college admissions process. As we continue to stay abreast of changes in college admissions trends, we recognize that every student has unique talents and interests. With that in mind we design individualized plans to fit the needs of our clients based on their academic and personal aspirations.

Our knowledge of a wide array of colleges and universities helps us successfully motivate and support our families step-by-step in navigating the college process as we find schools that best fit each student.

Our ultimate gift is watching each student thrive as a young adult as they make one of the most important decisions of their lives choosing the "Right Fit School!" We welcome the opportunity to be your family guide in this incredible college admissions journey!

Suited 4 Success
College Planning Services
Website: www.suited4success.org
Email: info@suited4success.org
Follow us on social media:
Facebook: Suited 4 Success
Twitter & Instagram: S4SCollegeBound
Office: 240-318-3468

Frequently Asked Questions

Suited 4 Success College Planning Services

What are the benefits of using Suited 4 Success over my high school's resources or over navigating the process?
The average public school counselor is responsible for 450+ students each year. Suited 4 Success will help in navigating the process as we provide you with guidance specifically catered to your individual interests and experiences. With 4000+ colleges and universities in the U.S., it can be difficult to fully explore all of your options. Suited 4 Success will guide you through the process with hands-on counseling via email, telephone and face-to-face assistance in order to ease the stress of the application process and ensure you are aware of all deadlines and requirements.

When should my child start working with Suited 4 Success?
You are welcome to schedule an Initial Consultation for your student at any time, but Suited 4 Success programs for college-bound students begin in 9th grade.

Do you offer a comprehensive package to assist with completing the college application process?
Yes. We assist with all areas of the application process, including essay topic development, critique, proofreading, organizational assistance, selecting recommendations, preparation of activity lists/academic resume and maintaining an action plan to complete applications.

In addition to comprehensive packages, do you offer rates for specific areas of the process?
Although the best value is our comprehensive packages, we do offer a number of packages for those seeking assistance on specific areas of the college admissions process.

Can I afford Suited 4 Success?

We offer flexible payment options and the opportunity to customize your student's program, to help your family make the most of the Suited 4 Success experience.

I am not in the DC, Maryland, or Virginia area. Can I still use your services?

Absolutely. Technology allows our counselors the opportunity to work with students Globally, in person or virtually via computer, phone or email. All our students, regardless of location, benefit from our services.

I would like to schedule a consultation as soon as possible. How soon can I get an appointment?

Contact our office at 240-318-3468 or email us at **info@suited4success.org** to schedule an Initial Consultation. Prior to the consultation, your counselor will do an in-depth review of your transcripts, test scores, and student and parent survey.

I just have a few questions about my student. Can I talk to a counselor without an Initial Consultation?

We do not provide advice or guidance without a thorough review of your student's history. You are welcome to ask specific questions during the Initial Consultation.

Do you provide tutoring services?

We do not provide tutoring services, but we do maintain a list of outstanding tutors with wonderful credentials for both academic subjects and standardized testing.

Testimonials

Suited 4 Success
College Planning Services
Shining Stars

Janae Johnson
Class of 2015
University of Pittsburgh

Being a part of the Suited 4 Success Program was very beneficial to me. Ms. Robinson truly takes the time to try and get to know her students so that she can guide them into making the best choices for themselves. Before joining the program, I believed that I could handle the whole college application process by myself but after sitting down with Ms. Robinson I realized that was not the case. With Ms. Robinson I was able to discover schools that were right for me that I otherwise would not have looked at and I was able to eliminate schools that I was unsure of after learning more information on them that Ms. Robinson provided.

Although I sometimes tend to be indecisive and a little stubborn, Ms. Robinson stayed on top of me making sure I met my deadlines and checkpoints in order to get my applications in as early as possible. One thing I truly appreciate is having the opportunity for someone to look over my applications and essays. When it comes to reviewing applications you really do need an outside opinion other than your parents to make sure you are putting your best representation out there. With Ms. Robinson, not only did I have an outside opinion, I had the opinion of someone who took the time to know me and who wanted me to succeed.

Without Ms. Robinson's help I do not think I would have received as many scholarships as I did, including two full ride scholarships, one to the University of Maryland College Park and one to the University of Pittsburgh. For that reason I would like to thank Ms. Robinson for all that she has done and my mother for getting me involved in this program.

Silmena Johnson, Mother of Janae

I was glad my husband and I attended the Suited 4 Success college workshop. We were new and very naive about the preparation and process for college. We were interested in getting applications in on time and gaining information on scholarships, grants and financial aid. I decided the Suited 4 Success program would help our daughter tremendously. With someone else working with her on the deadlines, her eight applications were in before the due dates. We started hearing back from colleges in November. I am very proud of my daughter, she has received money from six of the eight colleges already and it's just the beginning of February.

Chad Johnson
Class of 2015
High Point University

Suited 4 Success has truly helped me in preparing for college. Ms. Robinson not only assisted me in selecting Universities, she also gave great advice and guidance. She helped conduct research on University applications as well as pushed me to create astounding essays. By connecting with me and sharing her experiences, she motivated, educated, and prepared me to enter the next chapter in my life. Ms. Robinson made the college application process 1,000 times easier than it would have been without her. She continues to assist and give me advice even after my acceptance and enrollment into High Point University. I am truly grateful to what she has done for me and I may not be where I am today without her.

Parents of Chad, Charles and Scarlette Johnson

S4S was a great assistance in preparing college applications, and conducting assessments to determine what colleges were best tailored for my child's learning style. Ms. Robinson provided Information on financial aid and stressed searching for opportunities for scholarships and money for college. She developed a relationship with our son, which included frank and honest communication therefore enabling our son, and us to receive an unbiased opinion and assessment of the colleges that are best suited to ensure our son is put in the best position to attain his future goals. In addition, after our son was accepted into the school of his choice, Ms. Robinson assisted with guidance for taking his freshmen college classes and strategies for time management throughout his college experience.

Malik Murray
Class of 2015
Widener University

Getting ready for college was an extremely stressful process. My grades were above average, but I can honestly say that Ms. Robinson was the main reason that I am currently enrolled into a University. She constantly made sure that I did everything necessary to be successful. I definitely recommend this program to all High School students especially seniors. Parents if your child feels like they don't need a program like this, make the conscious decision to sign them up like my grandmother did. Ms. Robinson will make sure they get into college.

Geraldine Murray, Grandmother of Malik Murray

I had such a difficult time with my oldest grandson in the college application process; I knew I needed help this time around. Ms. Robinson was a heaven sent. She helped me stay on Malik with all the things we needed to accomplish in a timely manner. Every time I called her, she would always promptly return my calls. She was always willing to help. I had invested into this program with the funds that I planned to go on a cruise with. It was worth every penny.

Alyia Williams
Class of 2015
Delaware State University

Suited 4 Success helped me prepare for my future. Ms. Robinson was always there to provide assistance for whatever I needed. She made sure I stayed on top of college deadlines and helped me stay organized. Without her I don't think I would have gotten into my top three colleges. She brought a lot of amazing people into my life to assist me with SAT and ACT preparation. She has been there through the whole applications process. I know I can always come to her if I need help with anything. I will be attending Delaware State University and Ms. Robinson is to thank for that. She truly is a blessing and I thank God for her everyday.

Teresa Williams, Mother of Alyia

Suited 4 Success not only provided my daughter the best opportunity to get into college, but also gave her the confidence that she needed to fulfill her senior year and college acceptance requirements. Upon meeting with Ms. Robinson during the introductory session, she was able to access my daughter's strengths and weaknesses. In doing so, she developed a plan of action that allowed her to successfully complete her senior year and apply for colleges. She also recommended a wonderful tutor that helped my daughter achieve the SAT and ACT scores needed for college acceptances. The end result from participating in the Suited 4 Success Senior Counseling Program was my daughter being accepted into three colleges. She is excited about her future and is much more organized and confident than when we started the program. We are truly grateful for Ms. Robinson and the Suited 4 Success Program.

Today Is Just The Beginning...

- Today is the day I embark on a new journey unlike yesterday, the day before, or any other day; it is in fact a new day

- Every day I strive to be a better version of me than the day before

- It's the lessons I learned yesterday that help make today a better day

- What can I do differently today; that will yield better results than yesterday

- Life has been tough, but I have learned lessons I will carry with me for a lifetime

- Today I take up my wings and fly, because tomorrow is filled with new experiences, lessons, and most importantly memories

- A leader is not someone who just leads, but one who allows their voice to be silent while their actions speak volumes

- When you feel like the load is heavy take a deep breath and remember your purpose

- Aim for greatness for any reason you miss the mark you will still be great

- Every day you wake up consider it an awesome day

- Live life to the fullest so when you reflect back you have no regrets

- Wishing is just that, a wish

- Don't just dream create realities

- Opportunity is not given it is made
- No matter how hard you fall just remember to get back up
- Never stop moving towards your destiny
- Life comes with a plethora of barriers you never anticipated; always remember to stay the course
- When failure comes knocking continue running the race
- Remember every mistake, barrier and failure you encounter along the way to your destination is just a detour, not a stop sign
- Dreams are discovered while your eyes are closed, but in order to make your dreams a reality it will require you to open your eyes everyday with the determination that achieving your dreams is possible
- The distance between your dreams becoming a reality will seem difficult along the way; you will experience some setbacks, defeats, and failures but within the process you will discover YOU
- Unveil your WHY – then wake up everyday determined to make it a reality
- Jim Rohn says it best; "You are the average of the five people you spend the most time with". Ensure that your friends today align with your future plans for tomorrow.
- Popularity doesn't equal success, originality does
- Align your values with your purpose; your commitment to your passion; and your destination to your why and the best is yet to come
- Know that the greatest risk in life is not taking risks
- I leave you with this question…what mark will you make on the world?

College Admissions Glossary

Accrued Interest: The interest that has accumulated since the loan proceeds were disbursed, or since the previous interest payment if there has been one already.

Academics: A teacher or a scholar in a college or institute of higher education.

Alternative Loans: Education loans made by lenders other than the federal or state governments- also known as "private loans."

Athletics: Physical sports and games of any kind.

Annual Percentage Rate (APR): The yearly cost of a loan, calculated on a percentage basis, that reflects all finance charges including loan interest and fees.

College Fair: Is a relatively recent phenomenon that consists of a collection of colleges and universities that communicate and provide information online during a specific timeframe.

Clubs: An association or organization dedicated to a particular interest or activity.

Community Service: Voluntary work intended to help people in a particular area.

Co-Signer/Co-Borrower: Someone who obtains a loan with another borrower. Both parties are legally responsible for repayment of the loan. Lenders' policies concerning notification of billing statements, delinquencies, defaults, and other information may vary depending on whether the lender considers the individual a cosigner or co-borrower.

Credits: The acknowledgment of a student's completion of a course that counts toward a degree or diploma as maintained in a school's records.

Credit Score: A number that represents one's credit-worthiness, the likelihood of that person repaying a debt and the degree of risk for the lender. The score may impact loan eligibility and interest rate.

Disbursement: A process of issuing (transferring) funds from a lender to a borrower, often through the school.

Disclosure Statement: A lender's legal statement sent to the borrower immediately after a loan is approved or disbursed, identifying the amount borrowed, interest rate, finance charges, other terms, and the borrower's repayment rights and responsibilities.

Dual Enrollment: Involves students being enrolled in two separate, academically related institutions. Generally, it refers to high school students taking college courses. Less commonly, it may refer to any individual who is participating in two related programs.

Enrollment Status: A school's designation of a person as an undergraduate or graduate student, and enrolled as a full-time, part-time, or less than half-time student.

Expected Family Contribution (EFC): An estimated amount of personal resources a student and family should have available and is expected to contribute toward the student's education expenses for an academic year, based on a federal methodology.

Grace Period: A period of time when a borrower is not required to make payments on a loan, typically between leaving school or dropping below half-time enrollment and entering repayment.

Grants: A sum of money given by an organization, especially a government, for a particular purpose.

Private Loans: Education loans made by lenders other than the federal or state governments – also known as "alternative loans."

Promissory Note: The legally binding contract provided by a lender that the borrower accepts, which describes the loan terms, conditions, and obligations for repayment.

Programs: A planned series of future events, items, or performances.

Repayment Term: The period of time over which the borrower will repay the loan terms, usually range from 10-25 years.

Satisfactory Academic Progress: In order to receive student financial aid, a borrower must maintain a certain level of academic performance within a given period of time, which is defined by the school.

Scholarships: a grant or payment made to support a student's education, awarded on the basis of academics or other acheivements.

Time Management: the ability to use one's time effectively or productively.

Tutor: a private teacher, typically one who teaches a single student or a very small group.

Made in the USA
Columbia, SC
18 August 2018